D0794466

BICENTENNIAL GAMES'N FUN

"Like It Was"

BICENTENNIAL

GAMES'N FUN HANDBOOK

Adah Parker Strobell
Associate Professor, Department of Recreation, University of Maryland

and

Recreation Majors, Past and Present
University of Maryland

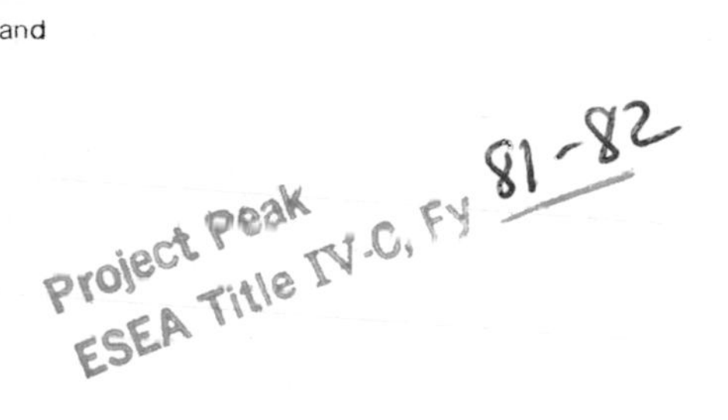

Preface by
Dwight F. Rettie
Executive Director, National Recreation and Park Association

Illustrated by Susan Walden

ACROPOLIS BOOKS LTD./Washington, D.C. 20009

ACKNOWLEDGMENTS

TO THE MANY RECREATION MAJORS at the University of Maryland, present and past, I extend heartfelt appreciation for your assistance, legwork, and enthusiasm. Special thanks are due the following people, who made this publication possible:

Richard Barr
Beth Berry
Linda Blakenship
Nancy Boone
Pam Brewer
Kendra Buckel
Carol Bullock
Roger Carlsen
Mary Ellen Carruthers
Ann Cavanaugh
Terry George
Mike Grossman
Mary Ann Haggerty
Davida Hall
Madalyn Johns
Ed Kowalski
Mary Kuchta
Vicki Loy
Donald Maier
Sharon O'Brien
Lida Payne
Regina Perrotta
Mary Phillips
Linda Pickwick
Beth Randall
Carla Rosenblum
Ernie Stieger
Susan Werner
Rebecca Wright
Noni Zollinhofer

Adah Parker Strobell

ACROPOLIS BOOKS LTD.
Colortone Building, 2400 17th St., N.W.
Washington, D.C. 20009

Printed in the United States of America by
COLORTONE PRESS, Creative Graphics Inc.
Washington, D.C. 20009

Library of Congress Catalog Number 75-18888
International Standard Book Number
87491-059-5 (cloth)
87491-060-9

Preface

IT IS HARD for many people to imagine what life was like without television and radio and rockets to the moon. For many people it is even hard to imagine what people did with their time when ready-made entertainment didn't exist.

Colonial America was, in many ways, a very harsh land. The struggle for bare existence must, by most of our standards today, have been grim. Roads were muddy tracks when it rained, work days were long, and the very existence of the Colonies precarious.

But the colonial era was also a time when people depended on themselves and their own imaginative bright spirits to bring joy and happiness to individuals and families. In our highly industrialized, sometimes remote society, the simpler joys of a simpler time have new appeal.

The American Bicentennial is a celebration—of our heritage from the past and our opportunities for the future.

This Bicentennial game book is full of the joyful heritage of games, dances, songs, crafts and recipes that brought fun and richness and a spirit of community to our colonial forebears. The book is for anyone who likes to share joy and creativity with people, both young and old. This book will be a valued resource for recreation professionals, teachers, parents, and volunteer leadership. It will not only help celebrate the American Bicentennial but it can enrich today's life with activities discovered from our past.

This book is the 32d edition of the National Recreation and Park Association's playground program series. NRPA is grateful to Dr. Adah Parker Strobell and her students, who are preparing for a career in recreation at the University of Maryland, for developing this unique publication.

Dwight F. Rettie
Executive Director
National Recreation
and Park Association

Contents

Introduction

WHAT DID CHILDREN of the colonial era do for fun? What games did they play, and what songs did they sing? What was everyday life like in the latter half of the 18th century? Every young person in this country deserves opportunities to learn about our American heritage, and to discover answers to these questions. As the nation's Bicentennial celebration approaches, it is especially appropriate that youngsters know about representative activities of our colonial forebears.

The colonists brought English, Scottish, Irish, African, German, French, Swiss, Dutch, Swedish, and other indigenous play forms with them. Many amusements were modified in the colonies. Other diversions, connected with barn raisings, hunting, farm chores, and other pioneer pursuits, were authentically "American," or were transformed into distinctly American forms.

There was not much regular contact between the major cities and developed areas of the Northern, Middle, and Southern colonies; culture was considerably less homogeneous than it is today and different geographic areas produced unique recreational patterns and activities. These in turn were shaped by climate, tradition, social mores, native industries, and many other factors.

Most colonial ways of having fun were passed down through word of mouth from one generation to the next. Others, such as recipes ("receipts") were sometimes transmitted in written form. Activities such as quilting and basket weaving were learned by imitation.

In gathering the material for this book, every effort was made to select "authentic" records or reconstructions of colonial pursuits and pastimes. In some cases, because of equipment required, safety hazards, or other reasons, modifications have been necessary.

We aimed for a varied and stimulating potpourri of programming ideas that could make colonial life "come alive" for today's youngsters—in effect, bridging two hundred years. If that happens, we've succeeded.

—Adah Parker Strobell

10

Games

This section presents a potpourri of colonial games and activities to please a wide variety of interests and diverse age groups. Activities for the "live wires," the "thinkers," and even the "social butterflies;" some to be played outside in a natural setting, other quiet games for smaller spaces, and even some social challenges for "get-togethers." Have fun!

12

1 Colonial Games

DURING THE "BICENTENNIAL ERA" there were relatively few games especially for boys or for girls; girls and boys played together for the most part. Often, the name of a game varied from region to region, and if the rules were written out at all it was done in an offhand manner. Some games, such as Cat Gallows, Honey Pots, and Shirking Walls, had specific names, while others were unnamed. Many games and sports originally played in different forms have evolved into such present-day activities as lacrosse, archery, boxing, cricket, and wrestling.

Americans of the Revolutionary era relied heavily on games they could devise using natural elements. The colonists adapted leisure activities from their native homelands and from their American Indian neighbors (lacrosse comes to us from the Indians).

THREAD THE NEEDLE
AGE GROUP: 5-12
PARTICIPANTS: Any number, but at least 10
DIRECTIONS: Each person holds hands with the person next to him or her in a line. All recite the dialogue: "How many miles to Babylon? Three score and ten. Can I get there by candlelight? Yes, there and back again. Then open the gates without more ado and let King Charles and his knights pass through." The player at one end of the line and the person next to him raise their two hands high to form an arch, through which the entire line passes; this repeats, with the whole group threading past each child. The players change places, so everyone successively becomes the "eye."

DUCK AND DRAKE (SKIPPING STONES)
AGE GROUP: 5-12
PARTICIPANTS: 2 or more
MATERIALS: Flat stones, shells, or a piece of tile for each player
DIRECTIONS: The objects are ricocheted ("skipped") across the water; the player whose object skips highest or longest wins.

PUSS IN THE CORNER
AGE GROUP: 5-12
PARTICIPANTS: 3 or more
DIRECTIONS: All players except one take positions around a room, for instance in the corners. One player stands in the middle of the room. The other players change places with each other in regular succession as the middle player tries to occupy a vacated position before another player gets to it; if he succeeds, the player who has been displaced takes the middle position.

HOP, STEP, AND JUMP
AGE GROUP: 5 or older
PARTICIPANTS: 2 or more
DIRECTIONS: The winner is the one who can,

by a hop, skip, and jump, cover the greatest distance from a given starting point. A running start is permissible, but the hop must start on a line.

CALL BALL
AGE GROUP: 5 or older
PARTICIPANTS: 3 or more
MATERIALS: Rubber ball; a wall
DIRECTIONS: The first player throws the ball against the wall, calling out the name of another player, who must catch the ball on the rebound. If he succeeds, he throws the ball next. If he fails, the first player throws again, calling another name.

COCK FIGHTING
AGE GROUP: 6 or older
PARTICIPANTS: 2 or more
DIRECTIONS: Each player stands on one foot and holds his other leg in one hand; all players hop around and bump into each other, trying to knock each other down. The winner of a round is that player who succeeds in knocking his opponents off balance, forcing them to let go of their foot, or making them place both feet on the ground.
VARIATION 1: Players hop on one foot with their arms folded across their chests.
VARIATION 2: Players squat, putting their arms around their knees and clasping their hands firmly; players hop, trying to unbalance each other.

TUG OF WAR
AGE GROUP: All ages
PARTICIPANTS: Unlimited
DIRECTIONS: *Distance method:* A long rope is stretched out on a level surface; each team grasps one end. A handkerchief is tied around the rope to mark its middle, and two lines are marked on the ground 4 yards apart and at right angles to the rope. The rope is stretched so as to bring the handkerchief midway between the two lines. On a signal, the teams pull; the winning team succeeds in pulling the handkerchief past the line.
Time method: Same as above, except that a single line is drawn under the handkerchief marking the middle of the rope, and the teams pull for 30 seconds. The team that is pulling the handkerchief past the line at the end of the period wins.
VARIATION 1: Stretch the rope on the ground, tie a handkerchief on it to mark its middle, and mark two finish lines at right angles to the rope, each 10 feet from the handkerchief. Set a starting line 50 feet from each end of the rope. The teams line up behind the starting lines and on signal rush for the rope and start pulling; the team that pulls the handkerchief across its finish line first wins.
VARIATION 2: Play as in distance method, except players pair up as horses and riders. The riders mount the horses, wrapping their legs around the horses' backs. The riders hold the rope, and at a signal the teams pull. Any rider who falls must let go of the rope until he is mounted again.
VARIATION 3: Players form a circle holding a rope, with the ends tied together. A line is drawn across the circle—all on one side of it constitute one team, those on the other side the other team. At a signal the teams pull, and the team that pulls the other over the line wins.
VARIATION 4: Two teams of players arrange themselves in file formation according to height behind the tallest player; each grabs the teammate ahead of him by wrapping arms around his waist. The two leaders reach over the starting line, and grab each other's wrists or a stick. The contest continues until one team has pulled the other over the starting line.
VARIATION 5: Two teams face each other from two parallel lines, with a 2-foot neutral space between them. A rope is extended between them at about waist level. At a signal all contestants push against the rope; the team that first pushes all the rope over the opponents' line wins.

PRISONER'S BASE
AGE GROUP: 8 or older
PARTICIPANTS: 6-40
DIRECTIONS: Players designate a playing area with agreed boundaries and a line dividing it into two equal parts. Two end lines are restraining lines. At each end definite prison areas are

established, not exceeding 4 by 4 feet. Two teams are scattered along the center line in their own half of the playing area. Players try to run through the opponents' territory to enter the opponents' prison, or to rescue a teammate who may be in the prison. As players are tagged they must go to the prison of the tagger. A tired runner may rest behind the opponents' end restraining line, but once he returns across the line he may not recross, nor enter the prison area, nor rescue a teammate until he has returned to his own territory. He may be tagged while trying to reach his own playing area. Members of each team guard their own prison. A rescuer may take only one prisoner with him. Both may be tagged while returning to their own area. Prisoners are not permitted to make a chain in order to approach an oncoming runner, and they may not step outside the prison area. A team wins (1) when it makes prisoners of all the opponents, or (2) when an untagged runner enters the opponents' prison while it is free of prisoners.

LEAP FROG RELAY

AGE GROUP: 8 or older

PARTICIPANTS: 10-40

DIRECTIONS: Players are divided into equal teams (no more than 8 to a team) and stand in file formation. Sufficient space is left between players so that each can reach his hands easily to the hips of the player in front. The first player in each file bends over by supporting his hands on his knees and ducks his head. The second player, placing his hands on the first person's back, jumps over him and immediately bends forward. Player three follows, jumping separately over the backs of players one and two and then bending forward. As soon as number one is the end man, he jumps forward over all the backs and then steps to one side. Number two follows and steps aside. Play continues until one team has no more players to be jumped over, and that team wins. Players should keep heads ducked until leap has been made, place hands between shoulders of persons over whom they jump, and jump with both feet, instead of pushing the supporting person.

SKIN THE SNAKE RELAY

AGE GROUP: 8 or older

PARTICIPANTS: 6-40

DIRECTIONS: Divide players into equal teams, no more than 8 to a team, and line up in file formation. Each player extends his left hand backward between his legs and at the same time grasps, with his right hand, the left hand of the player in front of him. At a signal, members of each file start moving backward. The rear player of each file, as the backward movement starts, lies down on his back, retaining the hand grasp with the player in front of him. The second rear player, after moving backward by straddling the last player, lies down, still maintaining the grasp with his two hands. The backward movement is continued, each player lying down after he passes over the other players by straddling them. When all are lying on their backs, the one at the rear of the file (the captain) arises and, straddling the prone players, moves forward, pulling the second player from the rear to his feet. This player pulls the third player. Action continues until all are on their feet once more. The team wins whose captain first returns all the members of his file to the standing position, provided no hand grasps were broken.

Each player, as he lies down, should keep his legs close against the body of the player in front of him, and turn his toes in. Players who are moving backward should move their legs well apart while straddling. Practice in slow motion before using as a race.

CATCHING A GREASED PIG

AGE GROUP: 12 or older

PARTICIPANTS: 1-10

MATERIALS: Lard; pig; rope

DIRECTIONS: Grease the pig with lard (or axle grease). Make a circle or "ring" on the ground with the rope, preferably in a soggy area. Contestants gather in the ring with heels against rope. On a signal they try to catch the pig, using various strategies. The game continues until the pig is caught; the pig could be awarded as the prize.

VARIATION: Send contestants into the ring one at a time and time the captures; the player who captures the pig fastest is the winner.

CLIMBING A GREASED POLE

AGE GROUP: 12 or older
PARTICIPANTS: Unlimited
MATERIALS: At least one pole; lard or axle grease
DIRECTIONS: Object is to see who can get to the top of the greased pole fastest—if indeed anyone can. A timer is necessary. Contestants begin from behind a line about 10 yards from the pole. On a signal they run from the line to the pole and begin their climb. They must touch the top of the pole to win.

JOUSTING

AGE GROUP: 9-15
PARTICIPANTS: 2 at a time; 2 spotters
MATERIALS: Sawhorse with padding (or gymnastics horse or Swedish box); 2 pillows; mats to cushion area around sawhorse.
DIRECTIONS: The object is to "kill" the opponent by knocking him off the horse with a pillow. Scoring is done by counting the best out of 5 tries (3 out of 5, etc.). Contestants may not hold on to any part of the horse nor move off a center line marked on the horse (this may be an imaginary line).

HOPSCOTCH

AGE GROUP: 5-12
PARTICIPANTS: 2-6
MATERIALS: A stick to scratch diagram into soft ground (or chalk for a paved surface); "potsie" (shell, pebble, marble, etc.)
DIRECTIONS: Each player must kick the potsie from square to square as he hops into it, starting at "1" and hopping up to "12" on one foot, then back again to "1" and out. In successive rounds he (1) carries his potsie on the back of his hand, (2) carries his potsie on his forehead, (3) carries his potsie on the small of his back (bent over), (4) carries his potsie on his right shoulder, and (5) carries his potsie on his left shoulder. If he ever kicks the potsie onto a line, drops it, or steps on a line, he is out until his next turn.

STILTS

Stilts are two poles that enable one to walk above the ground taking longer-than-normal strides. Stilts are of varying length and construction; each has a ledge, or footrest, where the foot is placed. Stilts may be mounted from a chair, a doorstep, a porch railing, or even a low branch. After mounting, the stiltwalker grasps the stilts firmly (normally at about rib height), and proceeds to walk by placing one stilt forward, then the other, and so on. At the outset, he'll probably find himself taking a few steps backwards and sideways, too! Soon, however, he'll gain control of his movements and may move forward rapidly and evenly, lengthening his stride with increasing practice

American Indians used stilts, mainly as children's playthings. Negro slaves reintroduced stilts in America through ritual dances.

The use of stilts is potentially dangerous. If used as a group activity, participants should be at least 12 feet apart (further if they are beginners). Younger children should begin by mastering mounting and balancing and then walking with control. Safety must be stressed.

Stilt activities could include stilt tag, follow the leader, stilt soccer, deep knee-bend contests, stilt dancing, "Simon Says," balancing contests, solo or group stilt hikes, and circle-filling contests (pack as many mounted stiltsmen as possible into circle drawn on *soft* ground—beware of "domino" effect).

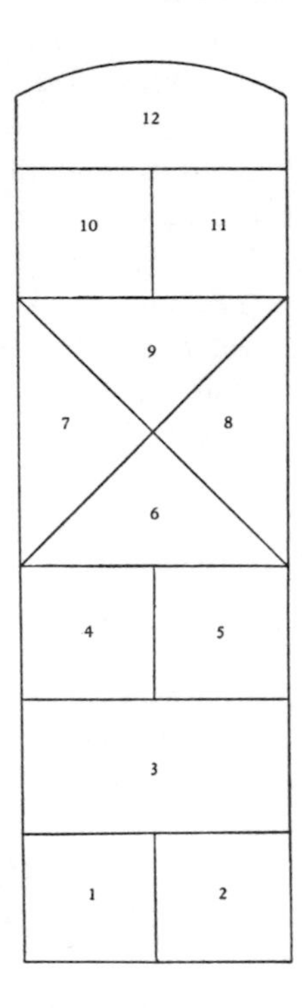

RINGER (MARBLES)—TOURNAMENT PLAY
AGE GROUP: 5-14
PARTICIPANTS: 2-6
MATERIALS: Smooth, level area for playing surface; round, clay playing marbles, 5/8-inch in diameter; round "shooters" of any substance except steel or other metal, between 1/2 and 3/4 inches in diameter

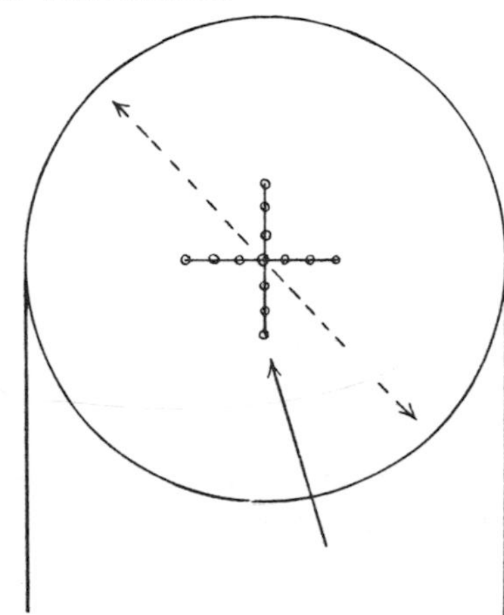

DIRECTIONS: "Ringer" is played in a ring 10 feet in diameter, with 13 marbles arranged in the center of a cross. The object is to shoot these marbles out of the ring; the player shooting the largest number in any game is the winner. All play is within the ring. With the center of the ring as a point of intersection, mark two lines at right angles to each other to form a cross, which will be a guide for placing the playing marbles. Place one marble at the center and three on each of the four branches of the cross, each marble 3 inches away from the next one. The "lag line" is a straight line drawn tangent to the ring and touching it at one point. The "pitch line" is a straight line drawn tangent to the ring, directly opposite and parallel to the lag line. The lag is the first operation in "Ringer." To lag, the players stand at the pitch line, or knuckling down upon it, and toss or shoot their shooters to the lag line across the ring. The player whose shooter comes nearest the lag line, on either side, wins.

Players must lag before each game; the player who wins the lag shoots first, the others following in order as their shooters lie nearest the lag line. The same shooter used in the lag must be used in the ensuing game. On all shots except the lag, a player shall knuckle down so that at least one knuckle is in contact with the ground, and he shall maintain this position until the shooter has left his hand. Knuckling down is permitted but not required in lagging. Starting the game, each player in turn shall knuckle down just outside the ring lag, at any point he chooses, and shoot into the ring to knock one or more marbles out of the ring.

A player continues to shoot when he knocks one or more marbles out of the ring, provided his shooter remains inside the ring. When a player's shooter passes outside the ring, whether or not he has scored on the shot, he doesn't cease shooting but is credited with the marbles he has scored. After a miss, a player picks up his shooter, wherever it lies, until his next turn, and then is permitted to take roundsters and shoot from any point of the ring lines.

ADDITIONAL REGULATIONS: Marbles knocked out of the ring are picked up by the player who knocks them out. Whenever a marble or shooter comes to rest on the ring line, if its center is outside the ring or exactly on the ring line, it shall be considered out of the ring; if its center is inside the ring, it shall be considered inside the ring. If a shooter knocks out two or more marbles in a combination play, he shall be entitled to all points on the shot. When a shooter slips from a player's hand, if the player calls "slips" and the referee is convinced that it is a slip, and if the shooter did not travel more than 10 inches, the referee may order "no play" and permit the player to shoot again. The referee's decision is final. The game ends when one player has knocked seven marbles from the ring.

SCORING: For each marble knocked out by a player, he gets one point. The player having the largest number of marbles at the completion of the game is the winner of that game. In the games where more than two players are engaged, if two or more players lead with the same score, those in the tie play a new game to break the tie. A player refusing to continue a game, once it starts, is disqualified, and if only two players are engaged, the game is forfeited to the offended player. The score of a forfeited game is 7-0.

BOWLS
AGE GROUP: 5 or older
PARTICIPANTS: At least 2—or 2 teams
MATERIALS: Two bowls (marbles) per person or 2 per person for each team; 1 jack (large marble)
DIRECTIONS: The jack is thrown by one of the players to form the "bull's eye." The players then in turn try to make their bowls come to rest as close to the jack as possible. After all bowls have been sent up (shot), the players try to determine which bowls have scored and which have not. This is decided by allowing all bowls belonging to one person (or team) that are nearest the jack to score. A round of 5 games is played and the higher-scoring team wins.

SQUAT (TAG)
AGE GROUP: 8 or older
PARTICIPANTS: Unlimited
DIRECTIONS: Children scatter over designated playing area. One player is designated "it" and tries to tag another. If he succeeds the tagged player calls out, "I'm it!" The only way a tagged player can avoid being "it" is to squat down and call out, "Squat!"
VARIATIONS: Instead of "Squat" a player may call out "Stone!" (as he touches a stone), or "Wood!" (as he touches wood). From time to time the leader may call out "No squats" (or "No stones or wood"), so that there is no way a player can avoid becoming "it."

CHIP STONE (or PEG A FARTHING)
AGE GROUP: 5-12
PARTICIPANTS: Unlimited
MATERIALS: Peg-tops, marbles, or coins (farthings)
DIRECTIONS: A small ring 1 foot in diameter is drawn on the ground. Each player places a marble in the circle. Players spin the tops outside the circle, pick them up in their hands still spinning, and try, by slipping the tops out of their hands, to knock the marbles out of the ring. Any marbles knocked from the ring become the property of the player knocking them out.

CHUCK A FARTHING
AGE GROUP: 5-12
PARTICIPANTS: 3 or more
MATERIALS: An equal number (2-4) of coins, stones, or soft drink caps for each player; a hole in the ground or a hat
DIRECTIONS: The players pitch their objects (singly) in succession toward the hole or hat. The player whose object lies nearest the hole has the privilege of going first. He pitches *all* his objects toward the hole or hat; those that go in are his. The player whose object lay second nearest the hole or hat takes the remaining coins and pitches them *en masse*—again keeping for himself those that go in. The game continues until no coins remain; the winner is that player with the most coins.

TRAP BALL
AGE GROUP: 8 and older
PARTICIPANTS: 2 or more
MATERIALS: Soft, small rubber ball, softball, or tennis ball; softball bat or stick; one trap or batting "T"

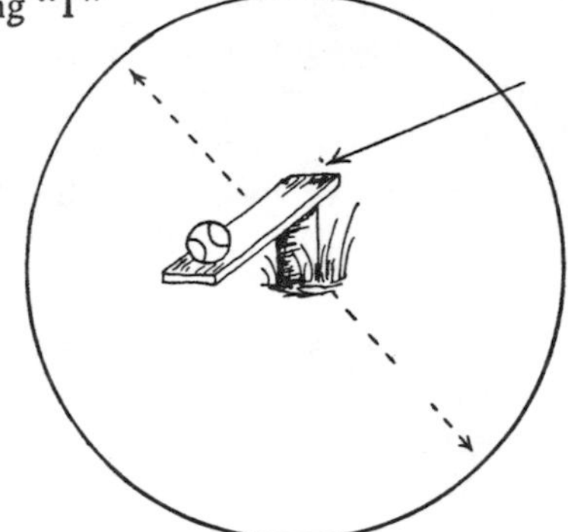

DIRECTIONS: A circle 20 feet or more in diameter is marked around the trap in the center. The first player (chosen by lot) steps up to the trap or batting "T" with a bat or stick in hand. He strikes the trap with his hat, releasing the ball. He must hit the ball with his bat while the ball is in the circle. The rest of the players stay outside the circle. If the player up at bat fails three times in a row to strike the ball out of the circle, or if he strikes the ball out of the circle but it is caught by one of the other players before it falls to the ground, he loses his turn, either to the next batter chosen by lot, or to the player who caught the ball. If the batter hits the ball outside the circle and no one catches it before it strikes the ground, the batter scores one point and continues at bat in succession, or is caught out. The highest-scoring player wins after all players have had their turn at bat or the time is up.

VARIATION 1: The batter drops his bat on the ground as soon as he has hit the ball beyond the circle. If the ball is not caught, the player who picks it off the ground may throw it at the bat inside the circle, from the spot at which he picked up the ball. If he hits the bat, the batter is out, and that player becomes the next batter up.

VARIATION 2: The ball may be thrown by a player chosen by lot, if no trap is available. Only the pitcher may catch the ball, *inside the circle*; if he is able to do so before the struck ball hits the ground, he may take his turn at bat. The other players must stay outside the circle, but may catch the batter out, as in the original game.

STOOL BALL

AGE GROUP: 6 or older

PARTICIPANTS: 3 or more (may divide into teams)

MATERIALS: A softball and a stool (or large carton)

DIRECTIONS: Set the stool or carton upon the ground and choose a defender, who takes his position beside it. The other players, called "bowlers," take turns toeing a line 10 or more feet away and pitching the ball at the stool, trying to hit it. Anyone who succeeds in hitting the stool becomes the defender, or batman. Any player, including the bowler, who catches the ball when it is batted back, also becomes the defender. The winner of the game is the player or the team that hits the ball the most times *before* it hits the stool.

BOWLING GAMES

The game of ninepins originated in Europe in the Middle Ages. It was brought by Dutch settlers to New York in the 1620's. Early ninepins lanes were made of clay or cinders. Later, a single plank about 1 foot wide was added, on which the ball was rolled. The pins were set up in a square formation, with one corner pointing toward the bowler. One of the earliest references to bowling in this country appears in Washington Irving's *Rip Van Winkle*, published in 1819, which speaks of the thunder of balls colliding with pins.

In the 1830's, the popularity of bowling had extended far beyond New York into many other parts of the country. However, its reputation came to be tainted as gamblers and criminals rigged matches and victimized those who refused to cooperate. Authorities in New York, Massachusetts, and Connecticut felt obliged to classify the game as a form of gambling and declare it illegal. The game of ten-pin bowling came about in part because of the edicts specifically proscribing "ninepins." The pin formation changed to a triangle, with the headpin facing the bowler.

KEEP AT IT

PLAYING AREA: playground or gymnasium

EQUIPMENT: one ball; 10 bowling pins

PLAYERS: Two teams, or multiples of two

Bowlers bowl one ball each in turn. All pins must be knocked down before they are reset. Thus, if a bowler leaves pins standing, his teammate following him bowls at the remaining pins. Each time the pins are all down a team scores one point. The play continues for a set period of time with the team having the most points at the end of playing time the winner.

STRIKE OR SPARE IT

PLAYING AREA: playground or gymnasium

EQUIPMENT: One ball; 10 bowling pins

PLAYERS: Two teams; any number

Each bowler may bowl two balls on each turn. If he strikes on the first, he has a chance to also strike on the second. If he fails to strike on his first ball, he can still spare on his second just as in regular bowling. For a strike, however, he receives 10 points and for a spare 5 points. The first team to score 50 points wins.

HIT THE CLUB

Players are paired off and may play singles

or doubles. Two Indian clubs are set up any distance apart, depending on the skill of the players. The player stands behind his club and rolls a volleyball at his opponent's club. Each time the pin is knocked down that player scores a point. The game may be a predetermined number of points or for a specified playing time.

BASKET BOWLING

The players try to bowl a softball into a wastebasket lying on its side, 40 feet away. Each team has from five to ten players; there should also be one player to act as retriever for each team. As the players bowl two balls in turn they rotate with their retriever. Each basket counts one point. Each player has five turns. Stepping over the foul line or bouncing the ball on the alley costs the player one point.

TIN CAN BOWLING

Six 1-quart tin cans are required. Punch holes in the bottom for drainage and sink them in the ground, level with the surface in this formation: one in the center, and the remaining five in a circle around the first, each 18 inches from the center. About 20 feet away, establish a bowling line. Ordinary croquet balls can be used. The players take turns, bowling two balls each turn. If a ball rolls into the center can five points are scored; the other cans score one point. Twenty-one points constitute a game.

HOOP ROLLING

AGE GROUP: 5-12
PARTICIPANTS: 1 or more
MATERIALS: 1 hoop and 1 stick per child
DIRECTIONS: Players line up in a row and race towards a predetermined finish line. Each drives and guides his hoop with a stick. Any player whose hoop falls to the ground is out of the game. The first player over the line wins.

HOOP DIVING

AGE GROUP: 5-12
PARTICIPANTS: 1 or more
MATERIALS: 1 hoop; a mat
DIRECTIONS: One player holds the hoop near the mat. The other player dives through without touching the hoop. Players change places so everyone gets one turn. The hoop is raised each round until everyone has missed (each player is out after his first miss). The player lasting longest wins.

STICK GAMES

Stick games of various types were common in colonial times, with cricket perhaps the most common. Such stick games as cudgeling and stilt racing were prevalent in Williamsburg, while "Zimba" was an Indian game utilizing sticks. Such modern sports as baseball, hockey, and lacrosse have evolved from these early stick games.

CRICKET

AGE GROUP: 8 or older
PARTICIPANTS: 5 or more
MATERIALS: wicket, bat, and cricket ball
The game of cricket played by the Virginia planters was different from the British national games developed in Hambledon in 1774. The wicket was two stumps or posts about a foot high and a foot apart, with a "popping hole" in the space between. The striker had to run to the popping hole and put the end of the bat into it before the wicket keeper could bowl the ball through the hole. The bat was similar to an old-fashioned dinner knife, curved at the back, and spiral at the front end. It was an instrument for hitting, not blocking. Since there were no set positions for members of a team, any number could play.

VARIATION 1: "Bandy." An old-fashioned game resembling cricket. A peculiar, shovel-shaped bat is used, flat and straight on one side and spoon-shaped on the other. The ball is bowled at the wicket, which is defended by the players. When the ball is struck, a run is scored by going to the base of the bowler and returning.

VARIATION 2: "Bandy." Players use sticks resembling large cricket bats to drive the ball along the ground in a game similar to hockey, except it was played in the streets (to harass adults, perhaps).

POISON STICKS

AGE GROUP: 8 or older
PARTICIPANTS: Unlimited
MATERIALS: 1 stick
DIRECTIONS: Choose someone as "it." The game begins when "it" chases whoever is holding the poison stick. The stick cannot be thrown but must be handed from one person to another. If the person being chased hands the stick to someone else, "it" must chase him instead. When anyone is caught carrying the stick, he becomes "it."

AMERICAN INDIAN GAMES

The games played by early American Indians reflected their lifestyles. They were simple and directly related to the skills needed for survival in different types of terrain. For instance, tribes living along waterways developed games in which the young were taught to be skillful in the water; woodland tribes developed games which promoted woodland skills.

The natural environment provided the equipment for Indian games. Logs, branches, stones, shells, and bones were used in many games. Balls were made from inflated sea mammal bladders. The spirit of competition and athletic skill was basic to most Indian games. Both individual and team competition can be seen in these games, and a sense of fair play was an important aspect.

THERE

AGE GROUP: 10 or older
PARTICIPANTS: 6-20
MATERIALS: blindfold for each child
DIRECTIONS: This game was popular with the Indians of the plains and the Northwest coastal areas. A circle of players is formed, about 50 feet in diameter. One player stands in the center blindfolded. A referee designates which player on the outside circle should proceed slowly toward the center man. The object of the "stalker" is to touch the center man before he can be detected. If the centerman points to the stalker, the referee indicates "right!," and the stalker must sit in that spot. The referee then points to another stalker to begin his advance. This continues until a stalker reaches the center man; if no one reaches him, the closest man to the center after everyone has had a turn is declared the winner.

OBSTACLE RACE

AGE GROUP: 12 or older
PARTICIPANTS: 5-10
MATERIALS: Logs, planks of wood, sheets, stones, barrels, etc.
DIRECTIONS: An obstacle course is set up, on either rough or smooth ground; objects might include sheets of cloth (to represent water), sacks and empty barrels to crawl through, and planks and logs to climb on or jump off. The player who successfully passes all obstacles and reaches the finish line first wins.

TOE-THROW STICK

AGE GROUP: 10-12
PARTICIPANTS: 2-10
MATERIALS: One 2-inch stick for each player
DIRECTIONS: Each player stands behind a line marked on the ground, with his stick balanced on the toes of one foot. It is preferable for players to be barefoot. The player then kicks his foot to send the stick travelling as far forward as possible. The place where the stick first touches the ground is marked; the player with the longest kick wins.

FIVE-STONE TOSS

AGE GROUP: 6 or older
PARTICIPANTS: 2-6
MATERIALS: 5 stones
DIRECTIONS: This game was played by Indian

girls of all ages. It is similar to the game of "jacks." Five stones are used, each about 1-1/4 to 1-1/2 inches wide. One stone is thrown in the air, while the others are scattered on the ground and picked up one at a time. If this is done successfully, the next sequence requires picking up one stone, then two stones, then the remaining one, and finally all four together. When one player misses, another player takes her turn; the first to complete the series wins.

SHINNY (ICE GAME)

Played in the northern regions of the continent. The game resembles modern-day hockey and was played by Indians of all ages and of both sexes, although in the Great Lakes region it was primarily a women's game.
AGE GROUP: Unlimited
PARTICIPANTS: Unlimited
MATERIALS: A 2- to 4-foot long stick of wood curved at lower end for each player; block of wood or ball of buckskin stuffed with hair; blankets or sticks
DIRECTIONS: Set up playing area on ice, 200 to 400 feet long with goals at either end made of blankets laid on ice (or two vertical sticks). A "medicine man" throws up the ball in the center of the field; on signal some start guarding the goals while others rush forward to score by pushing ball along ice with sticks. The first team to accumulate 4 points win.

WATER GAMES

SAFETY NOTE: A qualified lifeguard should be present during all water games and activities. No one should go further than he or she can swim back comfortably. If not using a pool make sure the water is approved for swimming and that all dangerous wildlife, protrusions, and weeds that could entangle feet are removed. There should be easy egress from the water and "spotters" to help lifeguard locate people in trouble.

CANOE TILTING CONTEST

Indian boys often played this game to practice boating skills.
AGE GROUP: 10 or older
PARTICIPANTS: 3 in each canoe
MATERIALS: Canoes; paddles
DIRECTIONS: Using their paddles as levers against the keels of the other canoes, one crew tries to tilt the opposing crews before its own canoe is tilted. The first crew to "dump" another canoe wins.

NOTE: A trained lifeguard should be present to referee; no players without Red Cross beginning level skills should participate. Paddles should only touch boats or water—not participants. Water must be over 5 feet deep and battle area at least 25 by 25 feet.

LOG RACING

AGE GROUP: 6 or older
PARTICIPANTS: 4
MATERIALS: 4 logs of the same size (size depends on ages of players)
DIRECTIONS: The object is to be the first to propel a log from one end of the swimming area to the other by paddling it.

RETRIEVING STONES (or DIVING FOR GOLD NUGGETS)

A favorite water sport of colonial children was throwing stones into creeks or ponds and retrieving them from the bottom.
AGE GROUP: 4-15
PARTICIPANTS: 100
MATERIALS: Olympic-sized pool; 10 cups; 490 pennies, 10 of which have been dabbed with gold paint
DIRECTIONS: Throw pennies in pool, distributing evenly. Divide 100 participants into ten teams of ten each according to swimming ability; each team has two nonswimmers as collectors. At the start each person sits on the wall at the area of the pool he can swim in. When the leader gives a signal each person slides into the water, collects one penny, takes it to one of his team's collectors, then goes back and repeats the procedure until all coins are collected. Each "gold" penny is worth 5 cents; the team with the most cents wins.
VARIATION 1: Use 490 pebbles painted gold and ten unpainted pebbles for the 5 cent bonus.
VARIATION 2: Ten participants in the swimming pool (or hole) with fifty gold-painted pebbles.

LEAF CONTEST

Each participant selects a leaf. On "go!" he places his leaf at a starting point (line) in the water; the first leaf to be carried by the current past a certain point wins.

VARIATION: Use sticks or crude whittled boats instead of leaves.

24

2 Parlor Games Charades, Forfeit Games, Cards, Backgammon, Word Games

IN COLONIAL TIMES, the parlor was the center of home entertainment, particularly for the upper classes. An evening might include musicales, card games, walks in the garden—and parlor games. These activities required little or no preparation; people of all ages—both family and visitors—participated. The two major types of parlor games were charades and forfeit games; the latter encompassed most of the games.

Charades, often known as "the game," was enjoyed early in our history and is still popular today. It consists of one person (or group) acting out or pantomiming words or phrases, while others guess the word or phrase being pantomimed.

In the 18th century special costumes, props, and musical accompaniment were used, in addition to actions and facial expressions. Apparently few official rules existed, except for commonly accepted conventions, such as choosing words or phrases that were not unreasonably obscure. As depicted in contemporary paintings and pictures, children also played charades.

"The game" is believed to have been brought from England by William Byrd, who learned to enjoy it there and introduced it to his Virginia friends upon his return home.

CHARADES

COLONIAL CHARADES

AGE GROUP: 5 or older

MATERIALS: Any impromptu props or musical instruments available

DIRECTIONS: Divide participants into two groups. Group A leaves room, chooses proverb or phrase and decides what props and pantomimes will be used. They return after an agreed time limit and perform their charade for Group B, which has set a time period in which to guess the proverb or phrase.

VARIATION: If a group guesses the proverb within the time limit, they are awarded a point; if not, the other team receives a point. At end of activity, the team with the most points wins.

USEFUL PROVERBS FOR COLONIAL CHARADES:

1. "All that glitters is not gold."
2. "A stitch in time saves nine."
3. "A fool and his money are soon parted."
4. "Every cloud has a silver lining."
5. "It never rains but it pours."
6. "Make hay while the sun shines."
7. "A barking dog never bites."
8. "Never look a gift horse in the mouth."
9. "A rolling stone gathers no moss."
10. "Better late than never."
11. "Birds of a feather flock together."
12. "A bird in the hand is worth two in the bush."
13. "Never put off 'till tomorrow what can be done today."
14. "A place for everything and everything in its place."
15. "It's better to have loved and lost, than never to have loved at all."
16. "What's good for the goose is good for the gander."
17. "He laughs best who laughs last."
18. "Out of sight, out of mind."
19. "Too many cooks spoil the broth."
20. "Rome wasn't built in a day."
21. "Where there's a will, there's a way."
22. "You cannot have your cake and eat it."
23. "Absence makes the heart grow fonder."
24. "The early bird catches the worm."
25. "Everything comes to him who waits."
26. "Laugh and the world laughs with you; weep and you weep alone."
27. "Idleness is the mother of evil."
28. "All's well that ends well."
29. "A new broom sweeps clean."
30. "It takes a thief to catch a thief."
31. "God helps those who help themselves."
32. "People in glass houses shouldn't throw stones."
33. "One good turn deserves another."
34. "All good things must come to an end."
35. "A friend in need is a friend indeed."
36. "To the victor belong the spoils."
37. "All's fair in love and war."
38. "Evil to him who evil thinks."
39. "Two wrongs do not make a right."
40. "Curiosity killed the cat."
41. "Necessity is the mother of invention."
42. "Variety is the spice of life."
43. "It takes two to make a quarrel."
44. "Nothing ventured, nothing gained."
45. "Handsome is as handsome does."

WORD CHARADES

AGE GROUP: 5 or older

MATERIALS: Paper and pencil to keep score

DIRECTIONS: Divide participants into groups of four or five. Each selects a word and takes several minutes to prepare pantomime. Groups then take turns presenting their charade to other groups. Talking is of course prohibited. If no one guesses the word, the performing group receives point; if someone does guess word (within time limit) their group receives point. Group with most points at end wins.

VARIATION: Use state names, flowers, birds, book or movie titles, etc.

ART CHARADES

AGE GROUP: 6 or older

MATERIALS: 2 pads of paper; 3 pencils or other markers.

DIRECTIONS: This game is similar to regular charades but instead of pantomime, drawings are used. The players are divided into two groups. Each group sends a representative to the leader, who gives him or her the title of a song, movie, book, or word from an announced category. The representative returns to the group and attempts to draw a quick sketch of the idea the word or phrase represents. The team to guess first raises their hands. No talking or actually writing out of words is allowed by the artist. A different representative is sent for the next word so the game continues. The team with the greatest number of correct guesses is the winner.

FORFEIT GAMES

These were extremely popular during the mid- and late 18th century. Many games ended with the redemption of forfeits. Usually as a person lost a game or was eliminated he or she gave up a small personal possession to the leader—a handkerchief, hair ribbon, etc. After almost everyone had at least one item to redeem they would choose a judge. The judge would sit with his back to the items and the leader would hold them over his head one at a time. The leader would say, "Heavy, heavy, hangs over your head." "Fine or superfine?" the judge would ask. "Superfine" the leader would say if the item belonged to a girl, or "Fine" if to a boy. The judge would then announce his decision of what the person had to do to redeem his possession. Performing the "penalties" was all in fun and there was no arguing over the sentence. Many forfeits were kissing penalties.

The first few games in this section are known to have been played during the latter part of the 18th century; the others are a sampling of more modern forfeit games. Almost any game where there are winners and losers can be adapted into a forfeit game.

HIDE THE THIMBLE

AGE GROUP: 5 or older
DIRECTIONS: Everyone leaves room except one person, who hides thimble somewhere in room. Others return and search for it; if it is too difficult the hider can give them "warm" and "cold" clues. The finder is the judge; everyone else must pay a forfeit.
VARIATIONS: After playing several times, anyone who hasn't found thimble at least once must pay forfeit, instead of everyone paying after first round. Or, for clues, use clapping—claps get progressively louder as searcher nears thimble, softer as he moves away.

UP JENKINS

AGE GROUP: Preteens to adult
MATERIALS: Coin; table and chairs
DIRECTIONS: Players divide into two teams, each sitting on opposite sides of table. Leader gives coin to first person in Team A and they pass it from person to person under the table! Leader calls "Up Jenkins!" and everyone on Team A raises closed fists over table. Leader then calls "Down Jenkins!" and everyone slaps their hands palm down on table. Team B then consults and tries to decide which hand coin is under. Only captain may speak; he points to different hands until he locates coin. For each hand pointed to that did not hold coin forfeit must be made.

TWENTY QUESTIONS

AGE GROUP: Preteen to adult
DIRECTIONS: One person chooses name of any object. Everyone else then asks questions trying to guess object. They are allowed 20 questions that can be answered, "Yes," "No," or "I don't know." Player answering keeps track of number of questions asked. At end of game, anyone who has not guessed word must pay forfeit.

BLINDMAN'S BLUFF

AGE GROUP: Unlimited
MATERIALS: Enough blindfolds for each participant
DIRECTIONS: One player is blindfolded while others find seats. Everyone then starts changing seats and person blindfolded tries to catch someone. After he has accomplished this, he asks captive a short question. Captive must repeat question three times, disguising his voice. If blindfolded person does not guess correctly whom he has captured, he must pay forfeit. Fresh blindfold is put on person captured and game continues.

BIRD, BEAST, OR FISH

AGE GROUP: Preteen to adult
DIRECTIONS: Everyone is seated in circle with leader in middle. Leader turns and points to one player, naming one of the three categories. Player must name member of that category before leader counts to 10. Names of animals, birds, or fish may not be repeated. If player cannot name one within time it takes leader to count to 10, he must pay forfeit.

HUNTSMAN

AGE GROUP: Preteen to adult

MATERIALS: Two rows of chairs, back to back

DIRECTIONS: A leader is chosen; everyone else takes a seat (any extras are removed). The leader gives everyone a name that is part of his hunting gear—coat, dog, powder, gun, etc. He then walks in a circle around the chairs and calls out different names or incorporates them in a story. As he says their object, that person gets up and falls in line behind the leader. After he has everyone following him, he sits down quickly and says, "Bang!" Everyone then finds a chair; the person left standing must pay a forfeit.

TONGUE TWISTERS

- Repeat three times with increasing speed:
  "Quizzical Quiz, kiss me quick."
  "Eleven elephants elegantly equipped stopped Eleanor's equipage."
  "Neddy Noople nipped his neighbor's nutmegs."
  "Peter Piper picked a peck of pickled peppers and put them on a pressed pewter platter."
  "Sam Slick sawed six slim, slippery, slender sticks."
- Repeat twice with increasing speed:
  I saw Esau kissing Sue.
  In fact we all three saw.
  I saw Esau, he saw me,
  And she saw I saw Esau.
- Read this rapidly but correctly:
  Esau Wood sawed wood. Esau Wood would saw wood! Oh, the wood Wood sawed! One day Esau Wood saw a saw saw wood as no other wood-saw Wood saw could saw wood. In fact, of all the wood-saws Wood ever saw saw wood Wood never saw a wood-saw that would saw wood as the wood-saw Wood saw saw wood would saw wood, and I never saw a wood-saw that would saw wood as the wood-saw Wood saw until I saw Esau Wood saw wood with the wood-saw that Wood saw saw wood.

SPEECHES AND RECITATIONS. Have people give 2- or 3-minute speeches on any of the following topics, or on any matter pertinent to the group:

- The political situation.
- The plight of the farmer.
- Pet peeves.
- The sex life of a stick of chewing gum.
- The importance of brushing their teeth.

Recite the following:

- Any passages from the Bible.
- Mother Goose nursery rhymes.
- Passages from Shakespeare.
- A favorite poem.

COMPLIMENTS

- Pay a compliment to five other people in the room.
- Pay three compliments to one other person.
- Say five complimentary things about yourself.
- Give five reasons why the ladies (men) admire you.

RIDDLES TO PERFORM

- Place one hand where the other can not find it (on the elbow).
- Leave the room with two legs and return with six (walk out and return with small table or chair).
- Ask a question that can not be answered negatively (what does Y-E-S spell?).

POSES AND IMITATIONS. Strike one of the following poses:

- Football player kicking a goal.
- Baseball player delivering a pitch.
- A small boy who has stubbed his toe.
- A timid young woman who has seen a mouse.
- A woman whose lap dog just died.
- Romeo looking up at Juliet, or Juliet looking down at Romeo.
- A small boy who has just caught a big fish.

Imitate one of the following situations or sounds:

- Three barnyard noises.
- A monkey eating bananas.
- Rip Van Winkle waking up.
- A concert pianist.
- A child giving a recitation.
- A back seat driver.
- An opera singer.
- Paul Revere.
- Someone singing in the shower.
- A small child taking castor oil.
- A politician warming up.
- A soap salesman, selling a new soap.
- Three bird calls.
- A barber shaving a customer.
- Humpty Dumpty's fall.
- A speedy typist.
- A tightrope walker.
- A ballet dancer.

ACTION STUNTS SUITABLE FOR THE PARLOR. Perform one of the following (make sure enough room is provided for balance stunts or big muscle actions):

- Hop across the room on one foot.
- Laugh, cry, whistle and sing in four corners of the room.
- Hop like a grasshopper.
- Yawn until somebody else does.
- March like a tin soldier.
- Dance a jig.
- Crawl across the floor on your hands and knees.
- Find somebody who isn't ticklish.
- Make three people in the room laugh.
- Hold a sofa pillow and sing a lullaby to it.
- Stand with back against the wall, stoop and pick up a piece of paper off the floor without bending the knees.

MENTAL GAMES

Many "standard" games of today have ancestral precursors that were played in colonial times. Some board games were played over 200 years ago by the Indians; other games were introduced by European colonists who brought some of their simpler board and table games with them to America.

The following are examples of games which we know were played by the colonists in the forms given or in similar versions. Modern-day games which have extensive or complex rules, strategies, etc., are listed rather than described.

CARD GAMES

FAN TAN

AGE GROUP: 7 or older

PARTICIPANTS: 3-8

MATERIALS: standard pack of playing cards; chips

DIRECTIONS: The entire pack is dealt. Depending upon the number of players, the number of cards in each hand will vary, some players having fewer cards than others. Each player must ante one chip before the deal, and after the deal each player with fewer than maximum cards must ante second chip.

The player on the dealer's left opens the play by putting a seven in the center of the table; if he has no seven, he must pay a chip to the pot. Thereafter, the play moves around the table to the left, each player putting out his sevens or building in sequence next to those already played. The four sevens are placed one above the other in the center of the table. To the left of a seven, the six of the same unit is played, and to the right the eight is played. Aces go next to the twos, and kings on top of queens. The player who lays down all his cards first wins the pot.

QUIET GAMES

EVEN ODD

AGE GROUP: 5-12

PARTICIPANTS: 2 or more

MATERIALS: Small objects (small enough to be hidden in hand)

DIRECTIONS: One player conceals a number of objects in his hand. Another calls "Even" or "Odd;" the pieces are then exposed and counted—if they correspond correctly to the odd or even call, the hider loses; if they don't, he wins.

CHESS

Chess is the most elaborate and characteristic of

all board games. It is probable that all card games owe their origin to chess, since cards themselves were derived from an old Indian variation of chess known as the Four Kings. It is said to have been invented in northwest India after the close of the Hun Domination, probably around A.D. 570. In its primitive form it was called Chaturanga. By the 13th century, the game was played all over Western Europe, and the modern format appeared during the 15th century. A major strategy game since its inception, the general character of chess is understood by almost every educated person in the world. Moslem chieftains used the game as a teaching aid to sharpen the strategical acumen of their officers. One ancient legend states that a pair of Eastern potentates staged a chess match rather than going to war since both were convinced the better game strategist would win the war anyway.

Following are just a few of the extensive publications and literature available concerning this example of a war game.

An Introduction to Chess Moves & Tactics Simply Explained. Leonard Barden. Dover Press, 1959.

Chess Fundamentals. Jose Capablanca. Harcourt, Brace & Co., 1921.

Chess, Beginner to Expert. Larry Evans. Lee Publishing, 1967.

Chess for You, the Easy Book for Beginners. Robert S. Fenton. Grossett & Dunlap, 1973.

Further Chess Ideas. John F. Love. G. Bell, 1965.

Championship Chess. P. W. Sergeant. Dover Press, 1963.

BACKGAMMON

Although chess, checkers and backgammon are all generally spoken of as "table games," strictly speaking, backgammon is the only game of Tables. It was in the early years of the 17th century that Tables became known as backgammon; arguments about the origin of the name are fierce and unconvincing.

Backgammon is an example of a race or track and pursuit game and is said to have been invented by an early Greek chieftain. Its board pattern is often found on the flip side of checkerboards. The game entails rolling dice to move 15 pieces off the board before your opponent does, but like many ancient games it has a deeper level of subtle skills in blocking or running opponents that can make it a high-stakes gambling game.

The following resources contain rules and strategies of the game.

Hoyle's Games Modernized. Lawrence H. Dawson. Routledge & Kegan Paul Ltd., 1971.

Foster's Complete Hoyle. R.F. Foster. J.B. Lippincott Co., 1963.

Hoyle's Games, Containing the Rules for Playing Fashionable Games. J.B. Lippincott Co., 1869.

DRAUGHTS (CHECKERS)

Checkers is so called only in this country; in England and the British dominions it is "draughts." See a standard rules book for basic English draughts, which we call checkers.

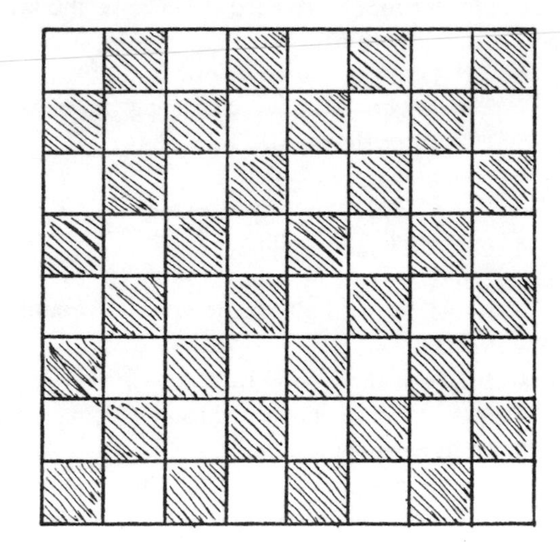

DIAGONAL DRAUGHTS

Standard rules for English draughts except that the pieces are arranged in the opposing corners on the board.

THE LOSING GAME

Each player has 12 men arranged in the conventional English manner and the moves and methods are the same, except that only the first penalty for failing to take an enemy piece applies. The opponent must insist that the piece which was moved be returned to its position and the proper capturing move be made. Each player to lose them all wins.

OTHER GAMES

GO BANG

Played on chess or checkboard by two people, each having 12-15 tokens. Lead is determined by drawing or agreement. Leader starts by placing token on any square he chooses. Opponent puts token on any unoccupied square. Each player then puts down one token in turn until all have been placed. If, while tokens are being placed, either player can get five tokens in line, horizontally, vertically, or diagonally, he calls "Go bang" and wins. When all men have been placed, players move alternately on unoccupied squares seeking to get in position. (Players should attempt to get three tokens in line with unoccupied spaces at each end.)

DOMINOES

It is believed that dominoes were derived, in ancient times, from dice. They have been played for many hundreds of years, and are still very popular. See a standard rules book for general rules and variant games, which include "Sebastopol," "The Draw Game," and "Bergen."

INDIAN JUMBLED WORDS

AGE GROUP: 10 or older
MATERIALS: Paper and pencil for each participant; blackboard or large piece of paper or posterboard
DIRECTIONS: Participants attempt to unscramble the letters in left-hand column to form words in right-hand column, all associated with American Indians.

MUMPAW	WAMPUM
LAPSC	SCALP
OWB	BOW
RAWHAPT	WARPATH
QUAWSS	SQUAWS
EPOPASO	PAPOOSE
OTMMTO	TOMTOM
RITEB	TRIBE
NAEOC	CANOE
AOHTAWMK	TOMAHAWK
ORARW	ARROW
PTEEE	TEPEE
ISOCMNAC	MOCCASIN
RORASIWR	WARRIORS

COLONIAL CATEGORIES

AGE GROUP: 10 or older
MATERIALS: Pencil and paper for each player
DIRECTIONS: Using one word, player must make a sentence, the initial letters of which spell the word. For example,

BOAT—Bob Owns A Tree

Score one point for each correct word (sentence structure must be correct).
Other examples:
REDCOAT—Running Everywhere, Dead Cats Operate A Tugboat.
COLONIAL—Can Oliver Lie Only Now In A Life Raft?
FLAG—Francine Loves A Guru.

THE RED, WHITE, AND BLUE

AGE GROUP: 10 or older
MATERIALS: Pencil and paper for each player
DIRECTIONS: Regardless of the number of stars, the colors in our flag remain the same—red for courage, white for purity, and blue for justice. Match the meanings in the right column with the color in the left column.

_a.	Red Cap	1.	British Soldier
_b.	Red Coat	2.	Caught in the act
_c.	Red Cross	3.	Memorable event
_d.	Red Handed	4.	National relief organization
_e.	Red Letter Day	5.	Porter
_f.	Red Light	6.	Professional hockey team
_g.	Red Tape	7.	Tedious official procedure
_h.	Red Wings	8.	Traffic signal
_i.	White Cane	9.	Burdensome possession
_j.	White Throat	10.	A symbol of England
_k.	White Cliffs	11.	A sparrow
_l.	White Collar	12.	Tuberculosis

_m.	White Elephant	13.	Mark of cowardice
_n.	White Feather	14.	Mark of the office worker
_o.	White Witch	15.	Symbol of blindness
_p.	White Plaque	16.	Guardian angel
_q.	Blue Beard	17.	Aristocratic lineage
_r.	Blue Blood	18.	Basic plan
_s.	Blue Book	19.	Insurance plan
_t.	Blue Coat	20.	Police man
_u.	Blue Cross	21.	Social register
_v.	Blue Laws	22.	Sunday legal restrictions
_w.	Blue Print	23.	Wife slayer

KEY FOR THE RED, WHITE AND BLUE

5a, 1b, 4c, 2d, 3e, 8f, 7g, 6h, 15i, 11j, 10k, 14l, 9m, 13n, 16o, 12p, 23q, 17r, 21s, 20t, 19u, 22v, 18w.

WORD GAME

AGE GROUP: 10 or older

MATERIALS: Pencil and paper for each person or team

DIRECTIONS: Using the word "Bicentennial," have players or teams attempt to find at least 20 words *in* the word. Rules: no plurals, at least 3 letters, no foreign languages.

TANGRAMS

Tangrams are a bit like jigsaw puzzles. However, instead of assembling the pieces to make just one picture, a tangram set can be made into hundreds of different pictures and shapes. These designs captured the fancies of American colonists in the late 1700's.

Tangram pictures are made from seven pieces (or "tans"), cut from a square. The tans are: two large triangles, a medium-sized triangle, two small triangles, and a rhomboid, a shapc resembling a leaning rectangle. (See illustration.) Use this pattern to make any size tangram set. Cut the seven pieces out of stiff paper or cardboard. The two equal sides of the triangle in the lower right corner of the pattern should be *exactly* half the length of the sides of the square. A simple puzzle to start with is to assemble your pieces back into the square without looking at the pattern.

To make a picture, all seven tans must be used. One piece must not overlay another, though either side of the pieces may be used. See examples.

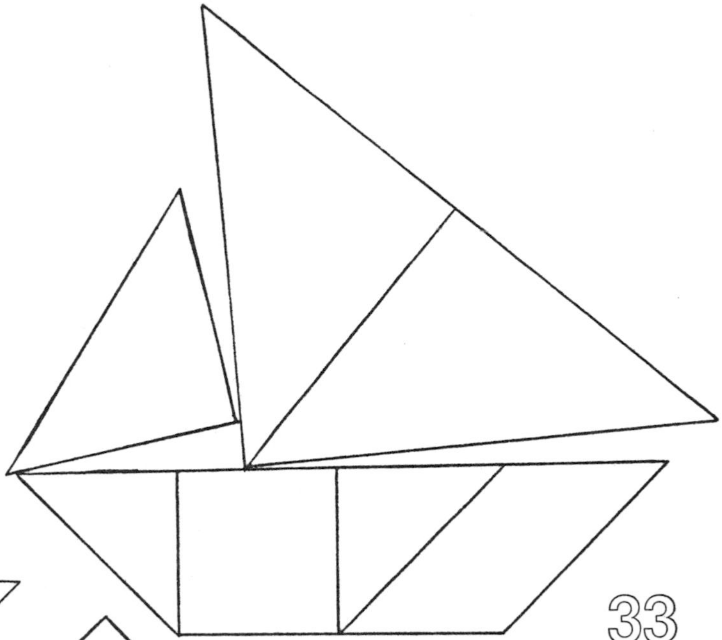

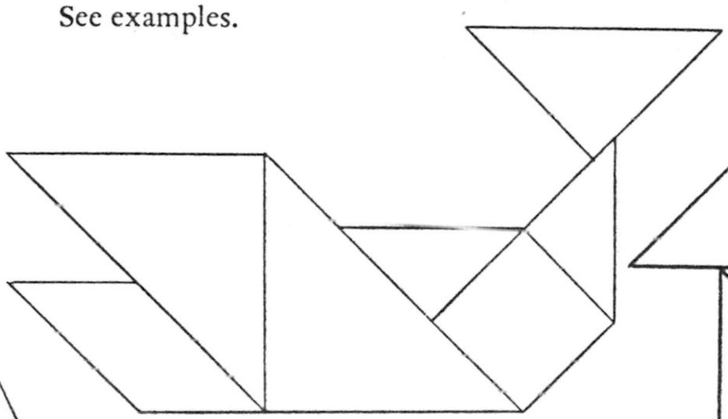

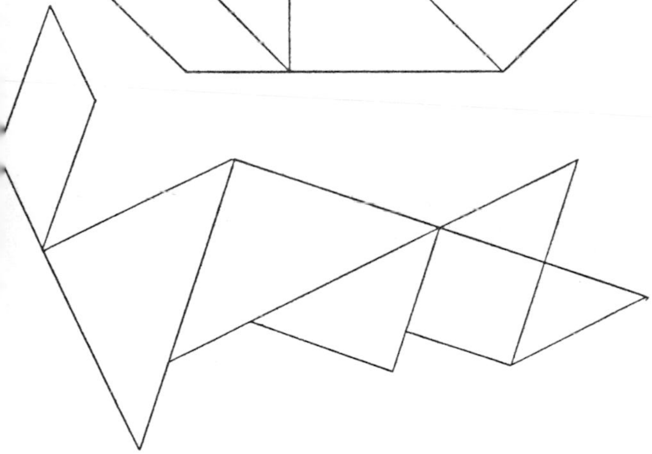

34

Toys

The few toys that colonial children had to enjoy were simple and made of whatever materials were close at hand. Playing with toys that children have made themselves certainly enhances the fun!

36

3 Colonial Toys

THE TOYS CHILDREN PLAY with often reflect the adult world in which they live. In colonial times, when adults worked hard and enjoyed relatively few amusements, toys were few and simple. Dolls were made of cornhusks, toy forts of corn cobs, and whistles of willow shoots.

Authentic folk toys give glimpses of the days when our ancestors were building a great country by hand, without power tools or giant machines. Hundreds of rural mountain families still spend their winters working on such toys, while they gather to tell the stories no one has yet written down.

With a few simple tools and the following basic supplies, many simple but interesting toys can be fashioned . . . like it was!

SUGGESTED MATERIALS AND TOOLS:

- Casein glue
- String or vines (honeysuckle or other pliable climbers)
- Wooden logs
- Wood chips, branches, acorn tops, nuts
- Chisels, screwdrivers, sandpaper

LOG ANIMALS

Kids will love these freewheeling pets! For the big pig, use a log with a flat side so casters can be attached directly to bottom. For hippo and little porker, nail a 3/4-inch white pine platform to one side (width should equal diameter of log so it won't tip). Hippo's body is about 12 inches long and head about 7 inches, with a slice of wood nailed between for a spacer. Chop out a triangular section for mouth and paint interior red. Use corks or small pieces of wood dowel for teeth, hosiery eggs for eyes, leather scraps for ears.

BALL AND CUP

A favorite pastime of the Court of Henry III of France was the ball and cup, or bilboquet. It is an excellent dexterity tester and pleasing toy for all ages. A ball of hard wood, an acorn, or similar spherical object is attached by string to a stem with a shallow cup at one end and a point at the other. The player holds the stem in his right hand and swings the ball, jerks it up, and catches it either in the cup or on the spike, which fits into the ball. Games can include the greatest number of successes in ten tries or ten minutes.

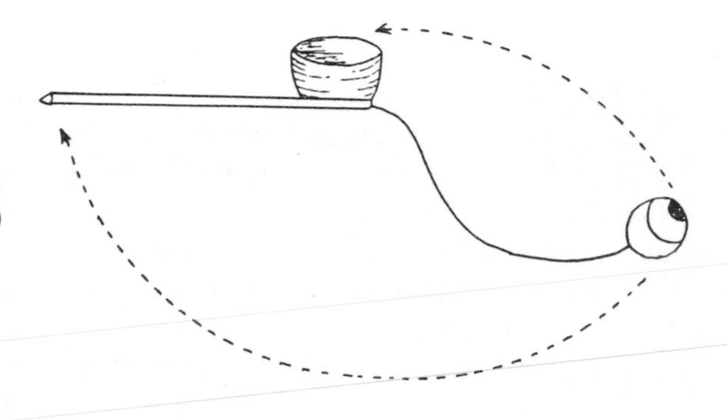

BUZZ SAW

The buzz saw toy is one of the simplest to make and enjoy. It consists of two short dowels or branches, a disc with two center holes, and several pieces of string. To construct it, thread the string through both holes and tie to dowels. To play, wind up the disc on the string by flipping and start an oscillating motion by pulling intermittently on the ends.

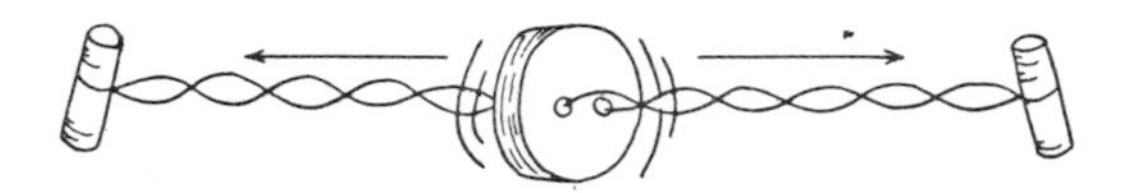

MOUNTAIN BOLO

Mountain bolo is another interesting skill toy. It can be made from string and several whittled wooden balls or round stones. To play, grasp the cord at center loop; by moving the hand up and down, try to make the balls orbit around in opposite directions.

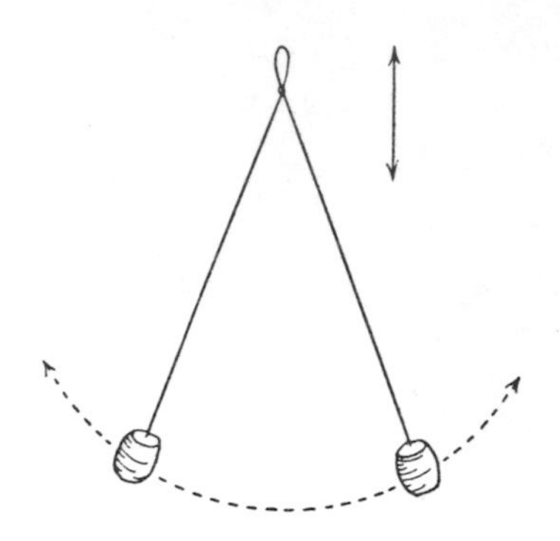

PLAY MOUSE

The play mouse is an interesting little toy. Using an acorn top, a hickory nut shell, some thin stems, and a small marble, children can fashion a miniature mobile toy that can be raced, admired, or used with other games. To make, take the top of an acorn and cut a round hole in the center. Hollow out a hickory nut shell or other shell of suitable size. Place the marble in the acorn top and put the shell over top. The hole should be big enough to allow rolling but smaller than the marble's diameter. To add the finishing touches, attach a sweet gum stem for a tail and the thin stems as whiskers.

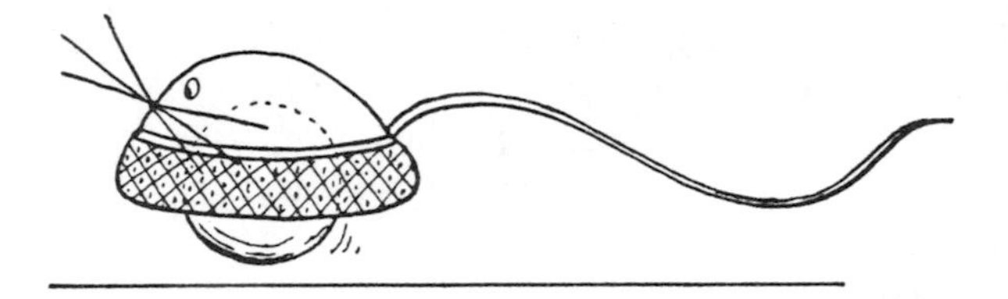

FLIPPERDINGER

This unique toy is made from elder wood, sumac, or river cane, hollowed out with a .22 caliber rifle cleaning brush. A light ball, made of cornstalk pith or plant core, and copper wire are also needed. Perhaps the most interesting application of this toy would be to test the breath control and power of smokers, but the toy is also great for individual and group fun. Put a piece of light guage wire through the ball and make a hook in the end. Fashion a hoop several inches up from the end of the pipe. Place the wired ball in the nozzle of the blowpipe. Blow gently on the pipe and the ball will float up. Try to snag the ball on the hoop; then blow again and try to unhook the ball and back it down into the pipe nozzle. To increase the difficulty, extend the copper wire hoops spaced consecutively higher. Attach point values for each level of accomplishment and conduct many successful hours of challenging fun.

40

4 Soaring with Kites

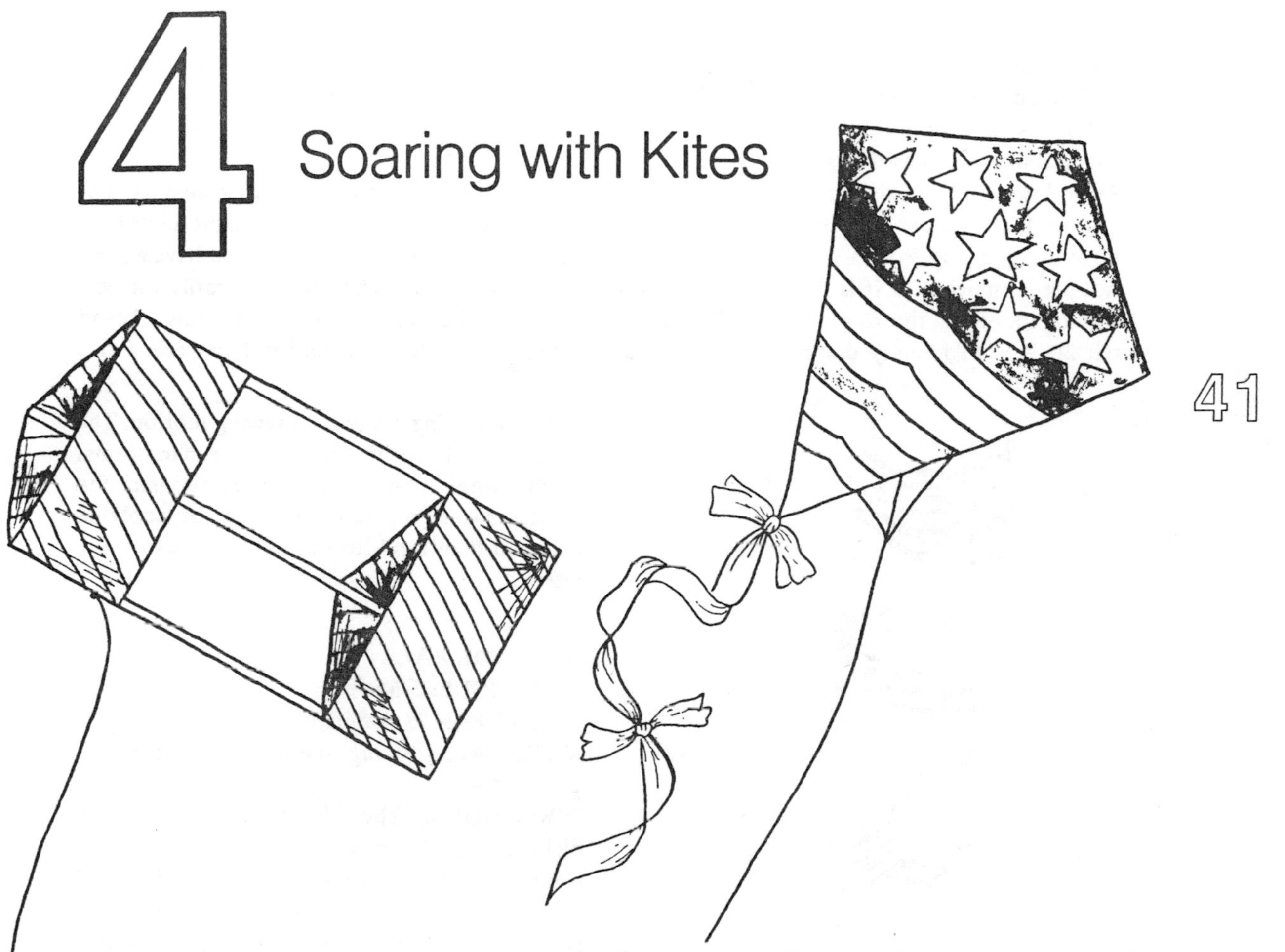

KITES HAVE AN UNCERTAIN history. Some believe they were invented about 2,400 years ago in Greece; others believe they originated in China. Almost everyone, of course, has heard of Benjamin Franklin's famous experiment involving a kite, a key, and a thunderstorm.

Anyone can fly a kite. Kites require minimal skill and are an excellent activity for many handicapped persons. Kites fly because they are inclined planes or flat surfaces, held up by the power of the wind. Part of the air moves over and part under the kite, creating a vacuum which lifts the kite. The key to kite flying success, therefore, is getting the kite properly angled in the air so that lift exceeds drag.

A kite will fly best when it has a light weight upon it. Try to get the kite up as quickly as possible. Have the string wound around a round object such as a stick, so it is easy to hold. This will allow for speedy release of the string while the kite is ascending into the air.

Standing in an open field or playground, release the kite. It should begin to drift upward; if it doesn't, hold the string roughly one foot from the kite and begin to run into the wind while gradually releasing more line. As the kite gains altitude, keep some line tension on the string, not so little that it loses wind power and falls, and not so much that it climbs too rapidly and loops over into a power dive.

When the kite has reached desired altitude, *gradually* stop the release of line. When the pull on the line feels gentle and the kite is flying evenly, more line can be released to the desired height. At times the kite may refuse to lift off the ground. This indicates that the bridle or the tail length needs adjustment.

Hand-winding a kite down can be a tiresome proposition. Not only do your hands get tired, but the increased wind power may cause the kite to "power loop" and fall to the ground. Try "walking down" the kite: simply tie the line to a tree or post and walk toward the kite, letting the line slide under your hands (if possible, wear gloves).

Some kites fly in an almost dead calm; others can withstand a gale. Ideally, an appreciable wind of from 6 to 15 knots per hour is best. Anything less means a lazy kite; anything more might damage it. Observe a flag flying from a flagpole—if it is flying straight out at a 90-degree angle, you have a good 9-knot-per-hour wind. If it is flying upward, the wind is too strong. March is not necessarily the best kite-flying month; in the Washington, D.C., area in 1973, August had 23 kite-flying days, July 21, and March 20. A cold January day may be ideal for kite flying: cool air has less density than warm and is easier to fly in.

KITE ACTIVITIES

KITE FIGHTING

AGE GROUP: 5-65
PARTICIPANTS: 2
MATERIALS: Kite string with abrasive surface; stable, maneuverable kite; reel
DIRECTIONS: In an open area such as a field with relatively few trees or other obstructions, each person launches his kite and takes a position 40-60 feet from the other person. The object is to cut the opponent's line before he cuts yours. This is done by entangling the lines and maintaining a vigorous sawing motion. The kites should be flown at lower-than-normal height. When a line is cut by the opponent, the game is over. Prepare the kite line by applying glue and then sand, to the 100 feet nearest the kite.

ALTITUDE RACE

AGE GROUP: 5-65
PARTICIPANTS: Unlimited
MATERIALS: Flying line; kite; reel (for each participant)
DIRECTIONS: The object is to reach the highest altitude in a designated time period. Contestants start on a starting line and have 5 minutes to launch their kites and return to the starting line. At this point, the judges, through a process of elimination, choose the kite with the highest altitude.

NOVEL KITE CONTEST

AGE GROUP: 5-65
PARTICIPANTS: Unlimited
MATERIALS: Homemade kite; flying line; reel (for each participant)
DIRECTIONS: The object is to design and decorate a kite, which will be judged according to construction, appearance, materials, and flying ability and behavior. Judges view first for

construction and appearance, then for fly-ability.

REELING-IN RACE
AGE GROUP: 5-65
PARTICIPANTS: Unlimited
MATERIALS: Kites; flying lines; reels
DIRECTIONS: Flying lines should be 100 yards long. The contestants launch their kites and upon a signal begin to reel in their kites. The first to reel in wins.

MESSENGER RACE
AGE GROUP: 5-65
PARTICIPANTS: Unlimited
MATERIALS: Thin, round pieces of cardboard with holes in middle; kites; flying lines; reels
DIRECTIONS: Thread a cardboard circle on each kite line. The object is to maneuver the cardboard disc up the flying line to the kite; the first to do so wins. The disc is propelled by the wind, according to basically the same principle as the kite.

5 Dolls of the Eighteenth Century

IT IS KNOWN THAT DOLLS, or something in the semblance of dolls, have been stirring the imaginations of children throughout human history.

Three hundred and thirty-four years ago the first doll was brought to America on the same ship that carried Captain John Smith. The oldest American doll in existence is one William Penn gave to his daughter in 1699. The doll is made of wood, overlaid with plaster, and is 20 inches tall. She has glass eyes and thick golden hair, and her dress is of striped and flowered brocade, a costume of the period.

Early American dolls form a cosmopolitan family, based as they are on European fashions of the period. Dolls that illustrate this to a high degree were called "fashion babies." Because colonial women couldn't consult fashion journals very easily, they had one-foot-high dolls arrive periodically from London and Paris dressed meticulously in the latest styles. The illustrations give some details that will help you outfit your favorite doll as a "fashion baby" of the colonial period.

TERMS

1. WATTEAU SACQUE: popular gown named for Antoine Watteau (1684-1721), who created the robe with a wide box pleat flowing from neck to hem or from neck to waist. The sacque often featured hooked panniers at the sides, and was worn over a quilted underskirt.
2. PALISADE: frilled cap to protect fashionable coiffure.
3. MOBCAP: woman's cap with a full crown and frills and fastened under the chin.
4. PANNIER: puffed overskirt.
5. RUCHE: a plaited, quilled, or goffered strip of lace net or the like used as an edging for collars, cuffs, and hems.
6. PALATINE: fur or fabric piece covering neck and shoulders, sometimes including a hood.
7. MODESTY PIECE: lace or lawn standing up across the front of a low-cut bodice that bared the neck, shoulders, and chest.
8. FICHU: an ornamental three-cornered cape worn by women on the head, neck or shoulders.

   TIPPET: a scarf of gauze, cloth or fur worn about the shoulders and chest for warmth and modesty.
9. CALASH: gigantic hood of silk shirred over a framework of whalebone used to protect high coiffures of powdered hair drawn ornately over a large cushion.
10. PELISSE: long outer garment.

1. Watteau Sacque
2. Palisade
Box Pleât of Watteau Sacque
3. Mobcap
4. Side Panniers
5. Ruching
—Under— Skirt
Milkmaid Straw Hat
Quakeress Cap
7. Modesty Piece
8. Fichu
6. Hooded Palatine
10. Pelisse
9. Calash

Fabrics were woven from linen, cotton, silk, and wool. They included muslin, chintz, satin, brocade, taffeta, lustring, lawn, gauze, lace, velvet, serge, and crepe. Leather, straw, false hair, fur, feathers, wood, fresh and artificial flowers, jewels, and cord were also used.

RAG DOLL

Rag dolls were usually extensions of simple, handmade efforts on pre-cut material in the shape of a doll. These were occasionally decorated with needlework and then stitched together and stuffed.

AGE GROUP: 6 or older

MATERIALS: Newspaper (for pattern); pencil; one-half yard cloth; needle and thread; stuffing; buttons; trimmings (rickrack, lace, ribbon, etc.)

DIRECTIONS: Cut a pattern roughly corresponding to illustration, from an 18-inch square of newspaper; each square on grid should measure 4-1/2 inches a side. Pin pattern on 1/2 yard cloth with sides together, and cut all around (see illustration). Start stitching at the side of the head; leave about 6 inches of top of head to allow for stuffing. Clip the seams. Turn right side out. Stuff the doll with shredded foam, polyester fiber, etc. With an overcast stitch, whip together the opening at the head. A mop of hair (yarn, felt strips) or a hat will cover the stitching. Glue or tack on facial features (or draw with felt tip pen), then dress as you will.

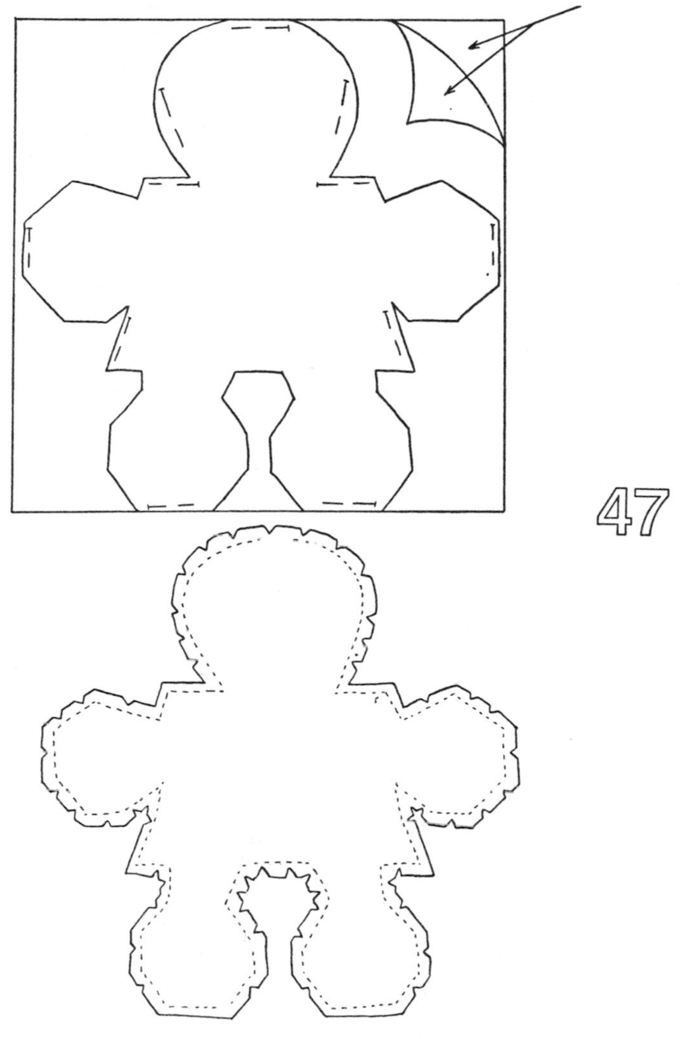

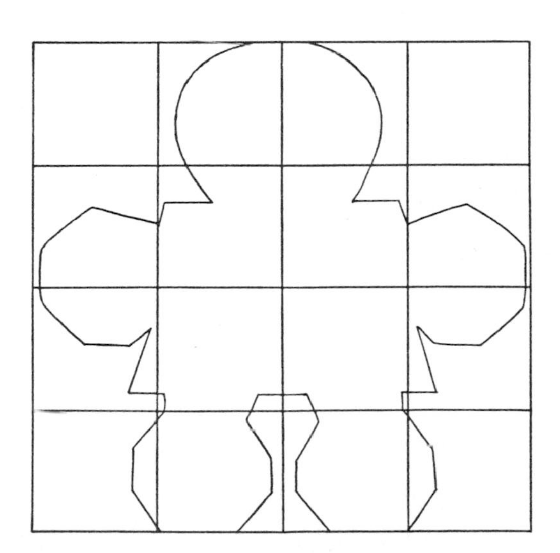

CORNSHUCK DOLL

AGE GROUP: 8-12

MATERIALS: Seasoned cornshucks; pieces of cotton; thin string; corn silk; large-eyed sewing needles; water pail

DIRECTIONS: Use as a late-summer project, when corn is in season. Shucks must be cured on the ear, so gather in late summer or early fall. Use inner layers; save corn silk for hair. Soak shucks in water for a half hour and keep them damp while working. Form cotton wad into ball. Take damp shuck and place cotton in center of it. Smooth stalk over the cotton and make ends meet. Tie string around shuck at base of cotton ball—head is now formed. Now take several husks and roll them so they are long and tube-like. Tie string to each end of lengthwise husk, forming arms and hands. Stuff cotton under the arm piece between the husks, then tie beneath with string; this will form bodice or chest. For girl doll, leave cornshucks straight to form skirt. Cover over the string with a piece of shuck about 1/2 inch wide and tied in back. For boy doll, split each end of the main shuck lengthwise up the middle; add more shucks, tuck them into the waist, and tie in place. Tie off the end of shucks to form feet. Hair: Glue or tie hair onto dolls, using corn silk or other materials. Make face using your own ideas and imagination. Let doll dry out in sun to prevent mildew.

ACORN DOLLS

AGE GROUP: 6-16

MATERIALS: Acorns; thread; strong needles

DIRECTIONS: Take acorn "caps" off and stitch together in long chains. Add cloth scraps to fashion into a man or woman doll.

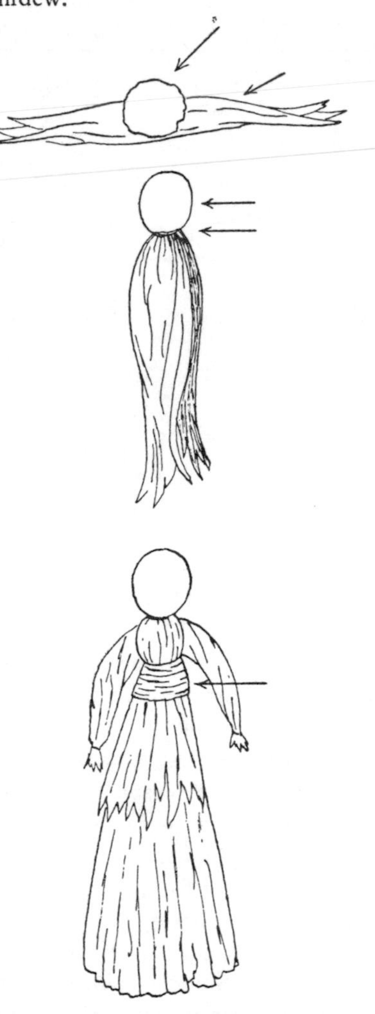

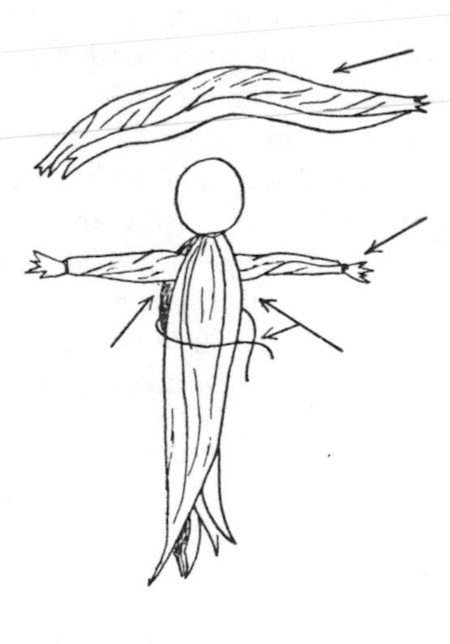

BOTTLE DOLLS

AGE GROUP: 6 or older

MATERIALS: Bottles with long necks; stuffing; string; cloth; paint; thread; needles; yarn or wool

DIRECTIONS: Pioneers used to create stories around these dolls for their children (or the children created their own). Take a fairly large piece of material and put enough stuffing in the center to form a head; tie at the neck, letting ends of material fall over side of bottle. Tie ends of materials to bottle to secure head. Tie a piece of string around the center of the head to give it a more contoured look. Wrap a triangular piece of paper (to draw face) or cloth (to paint face) around the head. Draw or paint face, and dress in colonial style. Arms can be made by either stuffing sleeves or cutting them out with material.

APPLE DOLLS

AGE GROUP: 8 or older

MATERIALS: Jonathan or winesap apples; rotating vegetable parer; pointed paring knife; ice pick or corkscrew; pipe cleaners; powdered sulphur; okra seed; glue; cuticle sticks; black eyebrow liner; mohair or cotton; hair spray; lipstick; rouge; clear nail polish; wire; nylon strips; invisible nylon thread; felt; fabric; small accessories

DIRECTIONS: Use peeled apples about 2-1/2 inches in diameter. Divide face into imaginary thirds. After features have been carved bore small hole in each apple and fill it with powdered sulphur to disinfect core. Brush with lemon juice and sprinkle with salt to prevent excessive darkening. Run pipe cleaner through apple from top, making crook at each end. Use upper end to hang carved apples in warm place to dry. Dry about 2 weeks, shaping if necessary to contour face or remove wrinkles. Wire for body must be strong enough for doll to stand yet supple enough for it to sit. Cut piece of wire 19 inches long, bend it in center to form a body and two legs; bend out feet at lower ends. Cut 9-inch piece of wire and place in bend of larger wire; wire two pieces together with very light copper wire at shoulders; this second piece forms arms. Bend loops at ends for hands. Head is fastened to body wire by pulling pipe cleaner hanger down through apple again, twisting two ends around copper wire tie. Pad neck with cotton and cover with nylon strips. Pad body wire with cotton until you have a good shape. Cover cotton with strips of flesh-colored or brown nylon. To give divided look to fingers and toes, make very tiny stitches with invisible nylon thread, pulling stitches up tight. Clothing: if dolls are going to a "meeting," use bonnets and matching dresses, lace-trimmed belts and buckles, etc. For a workday, use bonnets with aprons; give dolls paper shell pecan jugs or egg baskets to hold (or tiny Bible).

50

Drama

The whole gamut of colonial drama, the theater, stories and puppetry, was very different from what is known today. The stories that were told had a moral or religious purpose. The theater was not one of realism; continuous entertainment was presented, and the audience became involved with hissing and booing. Puppetry was presented for men as well as children and played a large part in colonial America.

6 Children's Stories

AT THE BEGINNING of the colonial era, most children's stories emphasized moral and religious precepts. By 1719 *Mother Goose's Melodies* had been printed in Boston; American children have loved these stories and fables ever since. *Robinson Crusoe*, published in England in 1719, and *Gulliver's Travels*, published in 1726, were popular adventure novels brought to America and read by many young people. *The Merry Tales of the Wise Men of Gotham* was issued in the colonies in 1755 ". . . to make Tommy a good boy and Polly a good girl."

Another well-known moralistic book for children was *The History of King Pippin* (1793), an account of the sad deaths of four naughty boys who were devoured by wild beasts. Maria Edgeworth's *Day of Misfortunes* is not so well known as her *Purple Jar* and *The Whip Cord*, but it is more applicable to a modern child's experiences, and represents the Edgeworth theories of childraising.

The Hymn in Prose, by Mrs. Sarah Kirby Trimmer and others, is representative of the work of a group of writers sometimes known as the Sunday School Group, of which Mrs. Trimmer was perhaps the best exponent. These writers strongly disapproved of fairy tales and were equally critical of "free thinking;" they emphasized instead religious principles and moral concepts.

William Roscoe's *The Butterfly's Ball* is noteworthy because it was one of the first children's books written with no morals attached. Following are brief selections from early American children's stories . . . like it was. They are adaptations of frequently told folk tales and history.

TWO FOXES

In a dark, busy forest in Virginia, where rabbits made eggs for Easter and toads make warts for silly folk, lived two foxes. They lived near a spring from which ran a little rivulet that gave water to the animals that lived in the woods. They were two very beautiful foxes. One was a little older than the other, and they were the best of friends. Their friendship was made of fire and water, the two great riches of the world, and nothing could break that friendship. Other animals in those woods gossiped about it, but just as barking couldn't harm the moon, all the gossip couldn't break the friendship of these two foxes. They went their way in peace and pleasure as God wanted them to live.

Yet, though the golden sun shines warm in the day, there is the dark night with cold winds. There was no end of animals and insects in the woods and the two friends saw and heard fussing and quarreling all around them.

One day the two foxes were talking pleasantly to each other.

"It is good to be like everybody," said the taller of the two. "Maybe we should try fussing and fighting, then we too will be like everyone else."

"Maybe you're right and we should be like all the other folks. I think I would like that," said the other.

"Come, let us start," said the taller.

"How do we start?"

"Let me think," said the taller. His long thick tail went down and so did his long snout. For a long time he was looking down on the little running water and the glittering stones lying around. "We could bite each other," said the taller. "I have seen many animals biting each other when they are angry."

"No, that would hurt," said the smaller.

"Yes, it would hurt. I am bigger than you and you are my friend and I don't want to hurt you. Maybe it would be better to get into an argument first and get angry at each other like everybody else."

"That would be better," said the smaller fox. "How do we do that?"

"Well here are two nice stones lying in the water; I'll show you how we start."

He picked up the two gleaming stones with his paws. Then, raising his voice, he screamed just as he heard the others do, "These two white stones are my stones, you can't have them, do you hear me!"

"Yes, I heard you," the other said. "If they are your stones, then they are your stones. I don't want to take anything from you. You keep them."

For a long time the tall fox was quiet. "We are not getting anywhere with our quarreling," he said, a little downhearted.

"No, we are not, good friend fox."

"Well let us try again. Let us try another way, maybe we can do better." They were quiet for a little time, then the older raised his long snout and bushy tail and said in a loud voice, "This wood belongs to me and you had better get out of it quick."

Said the other, "I am sorry, I like you and I like you to be my friend. But if this is your wood and you want it, I will have to go out even if I don't want to. It is a nice wood and I like it. Now I will have to find another."

The tall fox looked at his friend in surprise. He liked his friend and did not want to hurt him. "I don't want you to go. We are good friends and we like to be together and play with each other."

"I am happy to hear you say that. I didn't want to go, I want to be with you." The two were silent for a time, then the taller said, "Friend, we are not good at fussing and fighting and quarreling. I think it is best for us to be as we are, not the way others are."

So these two foxes in the deep wood remained, all their lives, good friends instead of fighting enemies. And I am glad they did.

NOBODY SEES A MOCKINGBIRD ON FRIDAY

Folks in Florida say nobody sees a mockingbird on Friday in the woods, and now I'll tell you why. But first I should tell you that the boys and girls of the state of Florida chose the mockingbird as the loveliest bird of the state, and with good reason. It is a very clever bird and can imitate the song of any other bird that sings, and even the whistling of people. One time a man who came from Europe said to the folks in Florida that the mockingbird did not sing as beautifully as their nightingale. They made a bet on that. The man from Europe went back and brought back some nightingales to Florida. The birds were let loose in the woods, and what do you think happened! The mockingbird soon imitated the song of the nightingale and sang even more beautifully.

But one day a week the mockingbird does not sing at all, and that day is Friday. Fact is, you don't even see much of that bird on Friday. Why?

Well, it is this way. Once there lived a very bad man deep in the Everglades or maybe it was up north in the Okefenokee. I don't exactly know where, but it doesn't really matter. He had a terrible temper and was at war with man and beast. He'd fight to shoot whatever man or beast came in his way. He was very strong, too, so that everyone was scared of him.

But there was some good in him, too. He loved birds, but the mockingbird most of all. He said the singing of that bird was much like himself. Sometimes it screamed harsh and croaking and then it sang so sweetly your heart would melt. He liked to sit on bright moonlit nights and watch the pale-gray bird with the long tail and the white patches on his wings singing sweet songs, screaming hoarsely, and imitating other birds. That man with the terrible temper would sit for hours listening. He'd break up stale bread to feed the mocking-birds, and sometimes they'd hop on his out-stretched hand for crumbs.

One day that bad man went a little too far with some good folks and they decided the best thing for everybody would be to get him out of the way. And that is what they did.

Everybody was glad that the bad man was gone, everyone except the birds, and most of all the mockingbirds. They were very sad. They flew all over to learn where he was, and in the end they learned he'd gone where it is hotter than any other place in the world. Then they were even sadder.

"We must do something about it," they twittered. "We must get him out of that terribly hot place!"

They went there by the thousands and tried to pull him out. But the fire burned their wings, and the heat and the smoke hurt their eyes, so in the end they had to fly away so as not to be burned altogether. But the mockingbirds weren't ready to give up.

"We must get our good friend out of there," they twittered all together. So they held a meeting.

"If we can't get him out of that terrible place, we can put out the fire so he doesn't burn," said the wisest bird. There was much talking and twittering, and in the end they decided the best way to put out the fire was with sand. They would fly to the shores of Florida and bring the sand from there, to put an end to the fire in that terrible place. That would save their good friend. They flew to the seashore by the thousands and, bringing grains of sand, dropped them on the fire.

But mockingbirds, like all creatures in the world, must build houses, take care of their children, and do many other things all of us do. So they had to stop flying to help their friend so as to do the other things that must be done. But they still wanted to help their old friend. Again they had a meeting of all the birds. There was much talk in mockingbird language, and in the end it was decided that the best thing was to take off one day each week and bring the sand to their friend. That day would be Friday. And so it was done and is still done to this day, for that hot place is a very big place.

Six days a week mockingbirds work at what they have to do and sing, but on Friday they fly off to the shores of Florida to get grains of sand to put out the fire in that hot place—to save their friend.

That's why you don't see mockingbirds on Fridays in the woods of Florida.

PRINCESS MARY OF MARYLAND

In 1634 curiosity arose in the Piscataway Village as Nicoatucen, the tribal messenger, arrived with news of the Great Canoe's approach. Uwanno, the emperor, and his brother Kittamaquund led the Piscataway tribe to the water's edge to meet the whitemen and to learn the reason for the visit.

Leonard Calvert, the first governor of Maryland, had come to ask the Piscataway Indians to protect the white settlers living near their village from other threatening Indians. It was agreed. Uwanno broke an axe and smoothed the rough edges with a stone, and Governor Calvert did the same.

Kittamaquund was happy. The peace agree-ment meant his daughter Little Girl would be safe from harm by invading whitemen. A few short years later Uwanno died, making Kit-tamaquund the new emperor. Because she was the daughter of the emperor, Little Girl be-came Little Princess.

Kittamaquund heard the preachings of Father White, a missionary who lived with the Piscataways. When he became ill, the Indian medicine men danced and sang songs to their gods, asking them to heal their emperor. But Kittamaquund grew worse. He sent for Father

White, who prayed over him and cared for him. Before long Kittamaquund was well. His cure at the hands of Father White confirmed his faith in Christianity, and he asked Father White to baptize him. A chapel was built in the village in preparation for the baptism. In attendance were Leonard Calvert, Mistress Margaret Brent and her brother Giles—both wealthy landowners of the county.

The ceremony fascinated Little Princess and kindled in her a desire to be baptized. This pleased Kittamaquund, but he also wanted his daughter to learn the English language and the whiteman's ways. So in the spring Kittamaquund took Little Princess to St. Mary's. Her first day there Kittamaquund discussed leaving Little Princess under Margaret Brent's care for one year. Kittamaquund left St. Mary's that night after Little Princess had fallen asleep. Little Princess awoke the next day to find that Kittamaquund had left her a present. It was Big Dog, the horse she had seen and liked so much on her journey to Mistress Brent's from the river. Big Dog made Little Princess happy and helped her forget her homesickness.

While at St. Mary's, Little Princess studied very hard and learned the English language. At the end of one year Little Princess learned of her father's death. She was grief-stricken but did not return to Piscataway Village. She continued her studies and was baptized. At her baptism she took the name of Princess Mary, and Margaret Brent named her Princess Mary of Maryland.

While she was at St. Mary's she grew close to Giles Brent and married him. They moved to Virginia where they lived in a large house and they had three children. Many times her children would ask her to tell them the story of Princess Mary of Maryland, so she would begin, "In 1634 curiosity arose in the Piscataway Village. . . ."

American Theatre, 1750-1800

THEATRE WAS A pastime for the few 200 years ago. Only people in cities, and primarily aristocrats, could attend legitimate stage plays. Yet in this period the seeds were sown for a significant American form of art and entertainment. The American Theatre has fluctuated between periods of overwhelming success and periods of near extinction. During colonial times the theatre was struggling for life; just as it was beginning to gather momentum, the Revolutionary War began and the theatre became one of the first casualties. The war was just one of the obstacles that confronted the theatre during the last half of the 18th century, yet the American theatre came into being during this period.

The year 1749 marks the first performance by a professional acting company in America, a troupe headed by Walter Murray and Thomas Kean. The conditions that Murray and Kean found in the mid-18th century were hardly favorable. The total population of the colonies consisted of about a million and a half white inhabitants and about a half million slaves, thinly scattered along the Atlantic seaboard from New Hampshire to Georgia Philadelphia, boasting a population of over 30,000, was the largest city; only three other communities were large enough to be called cities— Boston, New York, and Charleston. Ninety percent of the population was rural.

Transportation during colonial times was very poor. The few dirt roads that connected major communities were often very muddy in spring, blocked with snow in winter, and turning to clouds of dust in summer. Travel was slow, dangerous and generally unpleasant. Educational and cultural pursuits were confined to the aristocrats, for most of the colonists were too busy clearing the frontier and making a living to have time for anything but church-going. Although it was diminishing, the fanaticism that had brought on the Salem witch trials some sixty years earlier was still evident. Much of this fanaticism was directed at the theatre; every colony except Virginia and Maryland had laws forbidding the staging of plays.

The Murray-Kean Troupe and the acting companies that followed had their job cut out for them. With a small population scattered over a vast area, it was hard to assemble a sizeable audience. Since many of the colonists did not speak English, the audience was further limited. Poor transportation made it difficult for acting companies to travel from town to town, and inconvenient for people to get to the theatre. Add to these difficulties the Puritan and Quaker opposition, and one realizes what the early American Theatre movement was up against.

Little is known about the company headed by Murray and Kean except that it made its debut in Philadelphia in the fall of 1749 and moved in 1750 to New York, where it performed in a makeshift theatre on Nassau Street for a few seasons. The Murray-Kean troupe then moved to Virginia and later to Maryland, where it played in communities less hostile than those of New England. The troupe soon disappeared from the scene, apparently because it could not meet the competition of the famous Hallam Company, which arrived from England in 1752 and dominated the American Theatre scene for many years.

On the evening of September 15, 1752, the Hallam Company performed for the first time in America in Williamsburg, Virginia. They performed Shakespeare's *Merchant of Venice* before a packed house and were so well received that they extended their stay to nine months. In June 1753, the company moved to New York, where despite a complimentary letter from the Governor of Virginia, it took them three months to get permission to perform. They encountered similar opposition from churches when they arrived in Philadelphia in 1754. After receiving permission to perform, they enjoyed a very successful season.

With Mrs. Douglass as leading lady, with 18-year-old Lewis Hallam, Jr. as leading man and with himself as manager, promoter, diplomat, builder, and actor, David Douglass became theatrical king of North America for almost twenty years.

Between the time that the Douglass Company arrived in 1758 and the time it departed for Jamaica at the outbreak of the Revolutionary War, it accomplished much towards advancing the American Theatre movement. As the years went by, it presented a repertory of plays to growing audiences in more and more towns. David Douglass and his company were also responsible for building playhouses wherever they went—New York, Newport, Charleston, Annapolis, and Philadelphia. They had no choice. There were no other places to perform except taverns and vacant warehouses. The playhouses Douglass built were small, inexpensive buildings modeled after London playhouses. Two of the playhouses deserve special attention. The Southwark Theatre in Philadelphia, which opened in 1766, was the first permanent playhouse in North America. The John Street Theatre of New York, built by Douglass in 1767, was the scene of many historical firsts in the American Theatre. It was America's leading playhouse until the Park Theatre was built in 1798.

When the Douglass Company first came to the colonies, the troupe performed twenty-four plays. The repertory centered on plays of Shakespeare, but also included several modern tragedies and five comedies of George Farquhar. During their first year of touring they added six plays to the repertory, including *Romeo and Juliet* and *King Lear*. Each year, the company added new plays and subtracted some of the older works. There were no plays in the repertory written by native American playwrights. It was not until April 23, 1767 that the first play written by an American was presented by a professional company. Thomas Godfrey's *Prince of Parthic* was presented at the Southwark Theatre in Philadelphia by the Douglass Company, which by this time, because of political pressure, had changed its name to the American Company. The performance was a failure and it was not performed again. The event was significant, however, since the ice was broken for other American playwrights.

To grasp what the theatre was like two hundred years ago, let us imagine we are attending a performance in 1770 by the American Company. The theatre resembles other theatres we have seen; it has a lower floor or pit, a tier of boxes curving in a horseshoe from one side of the stage to the other and surrounding the pit, and a gallery above the boxes. Extending beyond the curtain line is a forestage. Proscenium doors on each side open on the forestage. Young women can be seen in the boxes trying to attract attention from the young men, a noisy crowd eating peanuts or apples is in the gallery, and the men in the pits are standing on the benches.

At last the stage manager blows a whistle, which tells us the program is about to begin. The musicians assemble in the narrow space in front of the stage and begin the overture. The audience reacts with a mixture of hisses and boos, along with a few apple cores flung from the gallery. The music stops, the crowd settles down and the large green front curtain is rolled up and the play begins.

The actors enter the forestage from the proscenium doors. Although William Douglass is playing the part of Othello and Mrs. Douglass is playing the part of Desdemona, their costumes are contempory. They represent neither the time nor the place described by Shakespeare. Since the players have to supply their own costumes, the inconsistencies of dress do not bother us. The scenery does not look real. A large cloth or drop with the appropriate background masks the back of the stage. Sometimes, instead of a backdrop, a pair of shutters—large painted flats fitted into grooves—meet in the center of the stage to form a continuous back wall. Concealing the offstage area on each side is a series of wing pieces parallel to the backdrop and painted to continue the same decoration. We have seen this scenery before in other plays performed by the American Company. Although the American Theatre has more than thirty plays in its repertory, it only has a limited number of wings, drops, and shutters. Since a taste for realism has not appeared yet, the artificial looking scenery, which is usually inconsistent with the real setting of the play, does not bother us.

During the interval between the acts one of the young actresses comes out, sings a patriotic song, and is met with a great burst of applause. It is the custom of the time to offer continuous entertainment, perhaps because there are no lounges in which to stroll, smoke, or converse. After the play there is an afterpiece, a farce which sends the audience home laughing and in good spirits. The handbill described this program as "a Series of Moral Dialogues in Five parts." Because of Puritan opposition, Douglass often had to resort to means such as calling his presentations "moral dialogues" and calling his troupe a "histrionic academy," denying that the activities performed had anything to do with drama. Sometimes his tricks succeeded; sometimes they did not. But Puritan opposition did not close this first period of the American Theatre; the Revolution did. In October 1774, the Continental Congress resolved that "we will . . . discountenance and discourage every species of extravagance and dissipation, especially all horseracing, and all kinds of gaming, cockfighting, exhibition of shows, plays, and other expensive diversions and entertainments."

The curtain came down and there was no professional theatre in America for almost ten years. However, during the war both American and British troops left records of giving plays.

After the war, the American theatre recovered and started a record of continuous growth. By 1784 the bulk of the American Company was at the Southwark Theatre in Philadelphia. Because the ban on theatres was still in effect, Douglass resorted to his old tricks, calling his productions "lectures," "moral dialogues," or "pantomimical finales." This angered the opposition, but Douglass succeeded. The company then moved to New York where it played a short season illegally. About this time many of the members of the American Company began to leave the troupe and start their own companies.

In 1789 Philadelphia repealed its anti-theatre law and Boston followed four years later. Once the Puritan and Quaker strongholds had surrendered, other communities quickly followed their example.

One of the most important theatrical events following the American Revolution was the emergence of influential American playwrights, for this was necessary for a truly American Theatre. Royall Tyler, educated at Harvard and Yale, became America's first successful native playwright. In 1887 he wrote a comedy called *The Contrast*, which premiered that year at the John Street Theatre in New York. It became a huge success and before the turn of the century it was performed in Baltimore, Charleston, Philadelphia, Boston and Richmond.

The Contrast is especially important for two reasons. Its appearance signaled the first literary theatrical movement in America: the Theatre of Sentiment. Like Tyler's play, many other plays written during this period emphasize American middle class ideals such as duty to God, country, and family, while lampooning the

British for their preoccupation with etiquette, manners, and other such nonsense.

In *The Contrast*, the American ideals of obedience and love of family and country are epitomized in Colonel Manly. Colonel Manly is contrasted with Billy Dimple, schooled in London and trained in English etiquette, who is involved in a scandalous relationship with three young women. He is engaged to Maria, but pursues Charlotte for his mistress and Letitia for her money. It is up to the audience to decide if the man of American principle is superior to the man with fine English manners.

The play is also significant in another aspect. In this play, the "stage Yankee" is introduced for the first time. Jonathan, Colonel Manly's servant, is the country lumpen, ignorant of the ways of the big city, proud of this ignorance, wanting only to return to his farm and his sweetheart. The "stage Yankee" was a device that American playwrights used again and again.

8 Puppets You Can Make

COLONIAL CHILDREN had few playthings because they were all handmade. Puppets weren't only playthings. Toy theatres traveled around the colonies, bringing entertainment in the form of drama and satire, mainly for theatre enthusiasts and mainly for men. Elocution and good speech were encouraged, and puppetry was a good educational tool, especially useful for religious beliefs. A Philadelphian described puppet shows in the 1700's this way: "These portable stages are of infinite advantage to most country towns where playhouses cannot be maintained. . . . The amusement is innocent and instructive, the expense is moderate, and the whole equipage easily carried about." In the 18th century puppet theatre played a considerable role in the public life of all countries, as indicated by the attacks it received from the regular stage.

Puppets may be operated from above, below, or from the plane of action. Operation may be by hand, strings, wires, sticks, or rods. It is difficult to be sure what kind were used in early American shows, but it seems that hand puppets and string puppets were both in use. How the puppeteer traveled had an effect; if by foot he probably carried simple hand puppets, and if by cart the more bulky string puppets. There was much influence from other countries. In 1771 hand puppets from Spain were used in New Orleans. In 1792 marionettes from England and Italy were seen in conservative Boston. In the 1790's shadow puppets began to be used. It seems, however, that the first puppets in America were brought through Alaska, for Indians used them to ward off evil spirits and never revealed how they moved. The Puritans outlawed puppets but got nowhere.

In the colonies puppet shows generally began at seven o'clock with the doors opening an hour earlier. Near the end of the 18th Century, a few started at six or six-thirty. Advertisements for puppet shows contain a great deal of information about shows of the period. One such ad appeared in the *Virginia Gazette* April 13, 1769:

> By permission of his excellency the Governor, for the entertainment of the curious, On Friday 14 April will be exhibited, at the theatre in Williamsburg, by Peter Gardiner, a curious set of figures, richly dressed, four feet high, which shall appear on the stage as if alive; to which will be added a tragedy called the Babes in the Wood; also a curious view of water works, representing the sea, with all manner of sea monsters sporting on the waves. Likewise fireworks, together with the taking of the Havannah, with ships, forts, and batteries, continually firing, until victory crowns the conquest. . . . The doors to be opened at four o'clock, and the entertainment at six. None can be admitted without tickets, nor any admitted behind the scenes,

as the inconvenience must be obvious. N.B. None of the above is represented by way of an optick box, or peeping through glasses, but shall appear publick on the stage, conspicuously to the view of the spectators, without confusion.

Puppets are fun for families and for groups of all ages. Here are some you can make.

PUNCH AND JUDY

Punch and Judy have changed so much over the years that it's difficult to pick out a specific representation and say, "This is from 1770," or some other colonial period. But the general idea is the same. They can still be made of wood today, by older children and adults. The wood should be a close-grained hardwood (fruitwoods are good). The basic tools needed are a vise, hand drill, carving knives, wood file, wood chisel, and hammer.

Outline head and bore hole in neck. Carve. Legs and body can be made of cloth. Blocks should be about 8 inches long, 2 inches wide, 1 inch thick for the hands. The block for the head should be 5 inches long, 3 inches wide, 3 inches thick for a puppet 15 inches or so tall. The body can be a sleeve from some piece of material with three holes. Make the body pattern about 15 inches long, 6 inches wide across the shoulders, and 7 inches wide at the bottom; put it on doubled material and sew. Tie and glue the arms securely. The puppet can be painted, fancily dressed, etc., or legs can be added.

A leg pattern can be drawn about 7 inches long. Two legs should be cut out on doubled material. If the legs are to bend at the knee, a seam should be sewn at the knee joint. Stuff with cotton. The feet can then be glued in place (doll shoes can also be used). The legs should be sewn about 4 to 6 inches below the shoulders.

These puppets are just like the figures used in Punch and Judy shows.

MARIONETTES—STRING-PUPPETS

Marionettes can be of varying difficulty. They can be made of anything from cardboard to wood. The colonists used wood, but some others are easier.

TISSUE MARIONETTE

MATERIALS: White or colored tissue; paper towels and masking tape; nylon hose; liquid starch—or dilute wheat paste with water; brush; shredded paper—newspaper or excelsior; telephone wire; scissors

DIRECTIONS: The body parts are made of little cushions strung together with telephone wire.

1. Make little cushions (fig. 1-2). Vary the sizes for head, body, and appendages. These can also be made by stuffing stockings. Wrap the cushions with strips of tissue (fig. 3-4).

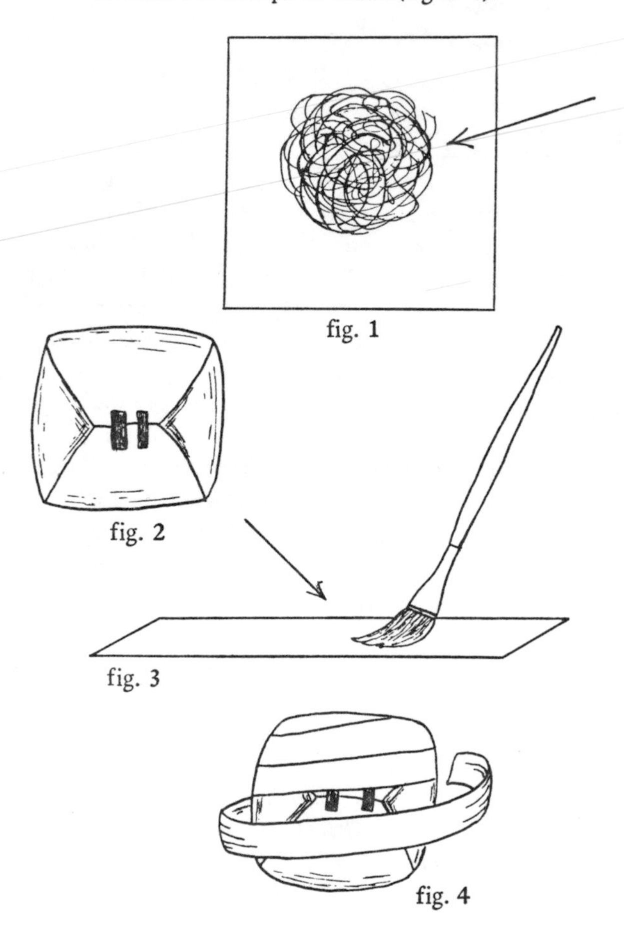

fig. 1

fig. 2

fig. 3

fig. 4

2. For facial features and other details wad bits of tissue, saturate with starch and apply to appropriate places. When dry they will be firmly attached.
3. Let these forms dry for at least a day.
4. To make moveable joints, make holes at appropriate points with hammer and nail.

5. Head connected to body by one loop of wire. All other joints connected by two loops of wire (fig. 5).

fig. 5

6. String puppet as shown. (fig. 6)

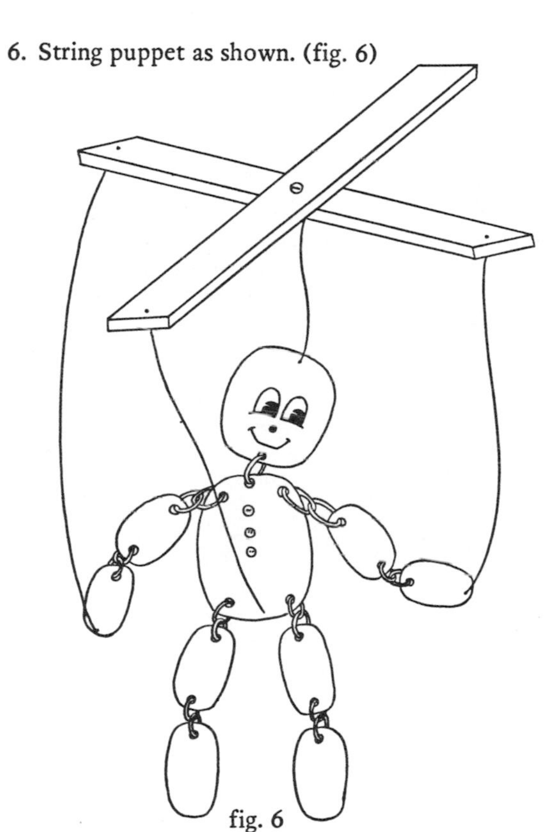

fig. 6

HOW TO MAKE AND OPERATE MARIONETTES

Carving from wood is difficult, so plastic wood could be used.

HEAD Model an egg-shaped head 3 inches high including neck from a piece of wood or a small can of plastic wood, forming the nose and eye sockets. After it's dry, paint desired features. Insert a small screw eye at the base of the neck and also where the ears should be after wood is hard (for attachment to the body and strings). Hair can be made. Shellacking may be done after the paint is dry.

BODY The shoulder piece is 1-1/2 to 3 inches across. The shoulder and hips should be 1 inch thick. Hips should be 1-1/2 by 2-1/2 inches. Insert a thick piece of wire at the base of the hip. Join the hip and shoulder pieces by a section of cloth which allows 1-1/4 inch between hips and shoulder. Cloth allows flexibility.

LEGS AND FEET Rounded soft wood is used. Joint is made of leather to allow for a bend. A section of leg is removed from the back on both so that the bend of the leg may be made. Small slots form the place for the leather joint to be tacked to. Leg is 2-1/4 inches long and lower section 2-1/4 inches. After joining two wood sections they are attached to hip wire by a piece of cloth. Attach cloth to the leg over hip wire to allow to swing freely (see diagram). Another piece of leather should be put at the bottom of the leg at the ankle. Feet can be molded from plastic wood (should be weighted with lead shot to help walking). Each knee gets small screw eyes and one at the middle of the back of the hip for strings.

HANDS Hands can be made of plastic wood or of wire with fingers covered with tape. A small hole at the wrist should be made for strings. The arms can be pieces of cloth attached to shoulder and hand. They shouldn't hang lower than 4-1/2 inches. Attach head by means of a wire run through another screw eye at top of shoulder piece.

When completed, make sure that a screw eye is placed on either knee, the middle of the back of the hip piece, and the head. Dressing and painting bring out the character of each puppet. They should be dressed in light materials such as silk or sateen and dressed as loosely as possible to allow flexibility.

CONTROLLING THE MARIONETTE

The device used to bring a puppet to life is called the controller. Two strips of wood form a cross. The main piece is about 9 inches long. At one end are two slits for the hand strings and at the other end one slit for the back string. The other cross piece is about 7 inches long; after being slit once at each end, it is attached by nails to the big piece 2-1/2 inches from the end. There is a small peg halfway between the smaller cross piece and the end of the long piece. Another piece of wood is the same length as the smaller one and has a hole bored thru its center to fit the peg. This piece is called the leg control and each end is fastened with two knee strings.

Head strings are attached first. They are attached to the smaller cross piece by putting the string thru the prepared slot. The back string is then attached to the long piece at the extreme end, and the hand strings to the opposite end. The leg strings are attached to the ends of the third piece. This allows operation of the hand and other controls separately from the foot controls.

A leather strap can be nailed to either end of one strip to hang the puppet up when not in use. Strings should be black silk fishline. String puppets are usually 30 inches long.

The main control is held in your left hand, and the foot control can be moved with the right. By tipping the foot controls up and down the legs will move as if walking. Walking is one of the most difficult feats to perform. By pulling on the hand strings the puppet will raise or lower his hands. By tipping the whole controller sideways, the puppet will bow. Operation takes practice; in time it will become natural.

The following publications offer additional information and ideas on puppetry and drama:

Do-It-In-A-Day: Puppets for Beginners. Margaret Weeks Adair. John Day Co., 1964.

Puppet and Pantomime Plays. Vernon Howard. Sterling Publishing Co., Inc., 1962.

Marionettes. Susan French. Reinhold Publishing Corp., 1964.

Music

A wide variety of dancing and musical activities are included in this section: singing games, the "leadup" to children's dancing, as well as play party games—perhaps the beginning of western square dancing; colonial popular songs for all ages; and how to make your own musical instruments for bicentennial celebrations.

66

9 Singing and Dancing Games

SINGING GAMES APPEALED to the children of colonial times because they involved physical movement, some play-acting, and merry tunes. Most of the original singing games were brought from English schoolyards and streets, though there is some evidence of Swedish, German, and Irish influence. These games were very popular in New England with children of all socioeconomic backgrounds.

The singing games were very informal; children enjoyed them because no supervision restricted their actions. The games were the children's daily recreation, learned not from formal instruction but from associates in the schoolyard or neighborhood. New singing games were introduced in an area by a visiting cousin or friend, who would return to his own community with new ones he had learned.

Younger children's singing games included "Round and Round the Valley," "London Bridge," and "Here We Go 'Round the Mulberry Bush," which are still popular today. Teenage girls enjoyed songs about their sweethearts or about courtship and marriage. These eventually led to kissing parties and the adult version of singing games, the play party games.

The subjects of the singing games varied but they all helped to carry the heritage and culture of the people. Children learned about other places and people, and even about their own background from these games. These singing games were molded by years of use and some eventually changed form. They were recorded only in the early twentieth century.

The following singing games represent a selection for different ages and can be enjoyed by all children. Singing games can be brought back to life again by children in schoolyards, streets, camps, recreation centers, and at home. They can help bring back part of our forgotten cultures, heritage, and customs, but most important they are fun.

ORANGES AND LEMONS

Or - an - ges and le - mons say the bells of St. Cle - mens

AGE GROUP: 6 or older

PARTICIPANTS: 10 or more

DIRECTIONS: This is played much like "London Bridge." Two players stand facing each other with hands joined forming an arch; one represents an orange, the other a lemon. The rest of the players, standing behind one another, each holding the skirt or shirt of the one in front, walk under the arch, turn to the left, walk through the arch again, turn to the right, and so on. All sing the verse shown. They continue singing, "Head, head," etc., until the child whom they want is passing under the arch; then they drop their hands over her head, take her aside and ask her which she will have, oranges or lemons. She chooses, not knowing which child represents oranges and which lemons, and takes her place behind the one representing whichever she has chosen. Meanwhile, the line stands still until the two children making the arch return to their places, and then continues walking through. The game continues until all have been chosen; a tug of war might ensue.

VERSE 1:
(On music)

VERSE 2:
When I grow rich, say the bells of Shore-ditch,
When will that be, say the bells of Stepney?
I do not know, says the old bell of Bow,
Pancakes and fritters, say the bells of St. Peter's.

VERSE 3:
Two sticks and an apple, say the bells of White chapel
Old Father Boldgate says the slow bells of Old Gate
Kettles and pans, say the bells of St. Anne's,
Pokers and tongs say the bells of St. John.

VERSE 4:
Brickbats and tiles say the bells of St. Giles
Here comes a candle to light you to bed,
And here comes a chopper to—
Chop, chop, chop, chop, chop, chop,
Chop off your head.

LAZY MARY

AGE GROUP: Elementary school age
PARTICIPANTS: At least 2
DIRECTIONS: This was usually acted out by two girls, with a singing chorus.

CHORUS:
Lazy Mary, will you get up,
Will you get up, will you get up?
Lazy Mary, will you get up,
Will you get up today?

VERSES:
Mary: What will you give me for my breakfast,
If I get up,
If I get up today?
Mother: A slice of bread and a cup of tea, etc.
Mary: No, Mother, I won't get up

Mother: A nice young man with rosy cheeks
Mary: Yes, Mother, I will get up

SOLDIER, SOLDIER, WILL YOU MARRY ME?

AGE GROUP: 5 or older
PARTICIPANTS: At least 2
DIRECTIONS: This was sung mostly by children and was a favorite amusement at afternoon gatherings. The object was to provide for the soldier the most varied wardrobe possible to entice him.

CHORUS:
Then away she ran to the tailor's shop,
As fast as she could run.
And bought him one of the very best,
And the soldier put it on.

VERSES:
Soldier, soldier, will you marry me,
With your knapsack, fife, and drum?
O no, pretty maiden, I cannot marry you,
For I have no coat (shoes, hat, etc.) to put on.

Soldier, soldier, will you marry me,
With your knapsack, fife, and drum?
O no, pretty maiden, I cannot marry you,
For I have a good wife at home.

FROG POND

AGE GROUP: 6-8
PARTICIPANTS: Unlimited
DIRECTIONS: The children sing the song, and represent frogs with a hopping motion. At the word "kough" they imitate the croaking of the frog.

VERSES:

Come, neighbors, the moon is up.
It's pleasant out here on the bank.
Come stick your heads out of the tank,
And let us, before we sup,
  Go kough, kough, kough.
And let us, before we sup,
  Go kough, kough, kough.

Hush, yonder is the waddling duck,
He's coming, I don't mean to stay.
We'd better by half hop our way,
If we don't he will gobble us up,
  With a kough, kough, kough.
If we don't he will gobble us up,
  With a kough, kough, kough.

THE MUFFIN MAN

AGE GROUP: 5 or older
PARTICIPANTS: 8 or more
DIRECTIONS: Form one large circle with hands joined, skipping to the left. A child stands in center and chooses a partner from the big circle by skipping toward the chosen one and offering both hands on the words, "Oh, yes we've seen the muffin man." The two occupying the center now join both hands and sing, "Two have seen the muffin man" to end of verse. At start of next verse, these two choose partners from the ring, and the four join hands, singing, "Four have seen the muffin man," etc., until all are chosen and big circle has sung, "All have seen the muffin man." (The two circles move in opposite directions.)
VERSES:

Oh, do you know the muffin man, the muffin man, the muffin man
Oh, do you know the muffin man, that lives in Drury Lane! Oh!

Oh, yes we've seen the muffin man, the muffin man, the muffin man
Oh, yes we've seen the muffin man, that lives in Drury Lane! Oh!

CHRISTMAS GAME

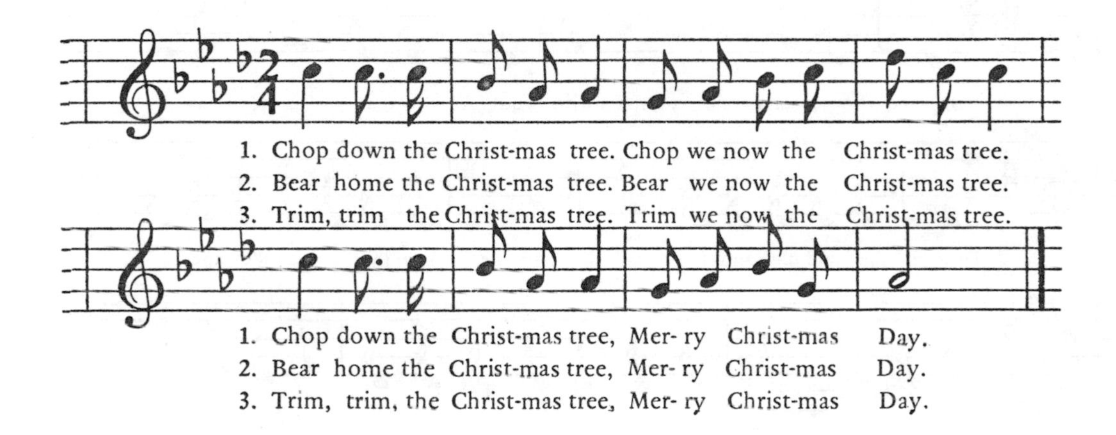

AGE GROUP: 5 or older
PARTICIPANTS: 6 or more
DIRECTIONS: This begins as a march, single file, the children in pantomime swinging axes with a long, sweeping motion. During the second verse they imitate the carrying home of the tree, dragging it or bearing it on their shoulders. At the beginning of the third verse a circle is formed and the pantomime of trimming the tree consists of reaching to the floor with one hand to pick up a gift or ornament, then stretching up as far as possible with the other to hang it on the tree. The last verse calls for a rollicking circle dance.

COFFEE GROWS ON WHITE OAK TREES

AGE GROUP: 10 and up
PARTICIPANTS: Large number of couples
DIRECTIONS: This is a Southern singing or play party game. Couples join hands with the ladies on the left, form a ring, and march around a lone man, who stands inside the circle. As they march, they sing the introduction in slow tempo. The man inside the circle chooses a partner from the ring. Then, while the dancers in the ring skip around him singing "Two in the middle I can't dance Josie," he swings his partner, first by the right hand and then by the left. Then the introductory stanza is sung again, while the dancers in the ring circle round and round and the two dancers in the middle each choose themselves a partner. All sing,

"Four in the middle and I can't dance Josie" while the two couples in the middle of the ring swing by the right and the left. The introduction is repeated, while all four dancers in the center of the ring choose partners. Then all sing "Wheel around and whirl around, I can't dance Josie," while the eight dancers now inside the ring break into groups of four and swing by the right and left. Then, as all dancers sing at a slow tempo, "Railroad, steamboat, river an' canal" six of the dancers inside rejoin the ring and all march around the couple that remains inside. They sing at a livelier tempo, "O she's gone, gone, gone . . ." to allow the couple remaining in the middle to swing right and left. The game then begins again with the introduction, skipping the first stanza this time, since a couple now stands in the center of the ring.

VERSES:
INTRODUCTION:
Coffee grows on white oak trees,
The river flows with brandy-o
Go choose some one to roam with you
As sweet as 'lasses candy.

1. Two in the middle and I can't dance Josie
Two in the middle and I can't get around,
Two in the middle and I can't dance Josie
Hello Susan Brown.

2. Four in the middle and I can't dance Josie,
Four in the middle and I can't get around,
Four in the middle and I can't dance Josie
Hello, Susan Brown.

3. Wheel around and whirl around, I can't dance Josie.
Wheel around and whirl around, I can't get around,
Wheel around and whirl around, I can't dance Josie
Hello, Susan Brown.

4. Fiddler's drunk and I can't dance Josie etc.
5. Briar in my heel and I can't dance Josie, etc.

Finale: Railroad, Steamboat river an' canal
I lost my true love on that ragin' canal
O she's gone, gone, gone,
O she's gone, gone, gone,
O she's gone, on that ragin' canal.

BETSY LINER

AGE GROUP: 8 or older
PARTICIPANTS: 5-6 couples per set
This is a singing version of the Virginia Reel to the Tune of "Ten Little Indians."

VERSES:

1. Bow down, old Betsy Liner (3 times)
   You're the one, my darlin'
2. Right-hand swing, old Betsy Liner (3 times)
   You're the one, my darlin'
3. Left-hand swing old Betsy Liner . . .
4. Both-hand swing old Betsy Liner . . .
5. Shake that right foot, get on around 'er . . .
6. Shake that left foot, get on around 'er . . .
7. Slide 'er up and down, old Betsy Liner . . .
8. Boy wouldn't swing, I wouldn't have 'em (alternating with "girl wouldn't swing") . . .
9. Moon and stars shinin' too . . .

FORMATION:

Two facing lines, boys in one, girls in other, about six feet between lines.

ACTION: (numbers correspond to verses above)

1. Head lady, foot gent, forward and bow, retire to places. Then head gent, foot lady do same.
2. Head lady, foot gent, advance, take right hands, turn around each other; same action for head gent, foot lady.
3. Similar action, using left hands.
4. Similar action, with both hands, turning clockwise.
5. Do-se-do is "back-to-back": each person folds arms, advances toward other, passes around other without turning around, back-to-back, and backs up to place. This time pass right shoulders.
6. Similar action, but with left shoulder for do-se-do.
7. Head couple join both hands, gallop sideways to foot and return with same sliding step to head. Then they link right arms and turn around one-and-a-half times, man going to the girls' line, girl to men's line, each offering left arm to line as they start to reel down line.
8. For swing verses, head couples reel to foot. For reel, partners link right arms in the center of set, then link left arm to next person, turn half-way around, back to partner in center, alternating between line and partner all the way down line. At foot, link right arm with partner once again, turn one-and-a-half times, come back to head, ready to lead lines to the foot. While this is done, two verses, "Boy wouldn't swing . . ." and "Girl wouldn't swing . . ." are sung alternately.
9. Each couple leads line in march to foot of line. There they form a two-hand arch. All other couples pass under arch, move toward head; this leaves second couple at head. Repeat until all couples have been in head position.

YANKEE DOODLE

AGE GROUP: 10 or older
PARTICIPANTS: Sets of 4
HISTORY: "Yankee Doodle" developed into an important song during the American Revolution. British soldiers sang a crude set of lyrics in order to mock the colonist soldiers; the colonists used another set of lyrics which became their battle cry. Yankee Doodle was a favorite with fife and drum. The colonists sang this song at their Concord victory (1775) and the colonial army sang it at Yorktown (1781) when General Cornwallis surrendered his sword to Washington. Doodle means dope, half-wit, fool.
DIRECTIONS: The dance derived from Yankee Doodle is as follows:
FORMATION:

Sets of four formed by two facing couples, women on the right. The whole group thus makes a double circle around the room. Partners hold inside hands.

FIGURE 1:

Couples advance and retire (measures 1-4). Women make half chain, offering each other right hands as they pass and giving left hands to opposite men who swing them into new place beside them (measures 5-8).

FIGURE 2:

Couples advance and retire (measures 9-12) with new partners. Men change, offering each other right hands as they pass (measures 13-16).

FIGURE 3:

Join hands in circles of four; advance and retire (measures 1-4). With hands joined make half circle to left of original places (measures 5-8).

FIGURE 4:

Couples advance and retire (measures 9-12). Drop partners' hands and pass through opposite couples, right shoulders to right shoulders (measures 13-16).

Repeat with new opposites as often as desired.

VERSES:

There was Captain Washington
Upon a slapping stallion
A-giving orders to his men
There must have been a million.

Then I saw a swamping gun
As large as logs of maple
Upon a very little cart
A load for father's cattle.

I can't tell you all I saw
They kept me such a smother
I took my hat off, made a bow
And scampered home to mother.

Troopers too would gallop up
And shoot right in our faces
It scared me almost half to death
To see them run such races.

CHORUS:

Yankee Doodle keep it up,
Yankee Doodle Dandy
Mind the music and the step,
And with the girls be handy.

THE BAPTIST GAME

AGE GROUP: 6 or older
PARTICIPANTS: Many couples
DIRECTIONS: This game was most popular in Virginia. The object is to switch partners, by playing a game similar to musical chairs. There is a row of couples, with an odd player at the head. At the (sudden) close of the song there occurs a mad rush and a change of partners.

VERSE:

The night is far spent, and the day's coming
on, coming on,
So give us your arm, and we'll jog along,
You shall be happy,
You shall be happy,
When you grow old.

10 Popular Songs

OUR MUSICAL LEGACY is rich and complex. Colonial settlers brought ballads with them from England and other countries. Slave ships from Africa were the source of other, different rhythms. Many French songs migrated to America via Canada, and Dutch, German, and Irish settlers further expanded the American songbook.

The first popular songs in this country were political, followed by hymns and other religious songs. Churches were extremely strict about which songs could and could not be sung in the parishes. Children's songs were often simple and crudely constructed.

In colonial times, only the texts of songs (lyrics) were printed; melodies were rarely included until after the Revolution. Singing was a popular diversion from the vicissitudes of colonial life.

The following, almost all folk songs, were sung in America in the middle and late 18th century.

MISTER RABBIT

VERSES:

"Mister Rabbit, Mister Rabbit, your coat's mighty grey."
"Yes, bless God, been out 'fo' day."
"Mister Rabbit, Mister Rabbit, your ears mighty long."
"Yes, bless God, been put on wrong."
"Mister Rabbit, Mister Rabbit, your ears mighty thin."
"Yes, bless God, been splittin' the wind."

REFRAIN:

Ev'y little soul gwine-a shine, shine,
Ev'y little soul gwine-a shine along.

GO TELL AUNT NANCY

VERSES:

The one she's been savin'
The one she's been savin'
The one she's been savin'
To make her feather bed.

She drowned in the millpond,
She drowned in the millpond.
She drowned in the millpond
Standing on her head.

Old gander's weepin',
Old gander's weepin',
Old gander's weepin'
Because his wife is dead.

The goslin's are mournin',
The goslin's are mournin',
The goslin's are mournin'
'Cause their mammy's dead.

She only had one feather,
She only had one feather,
She only had one feather
A-stickin' in her head.

THE FOX

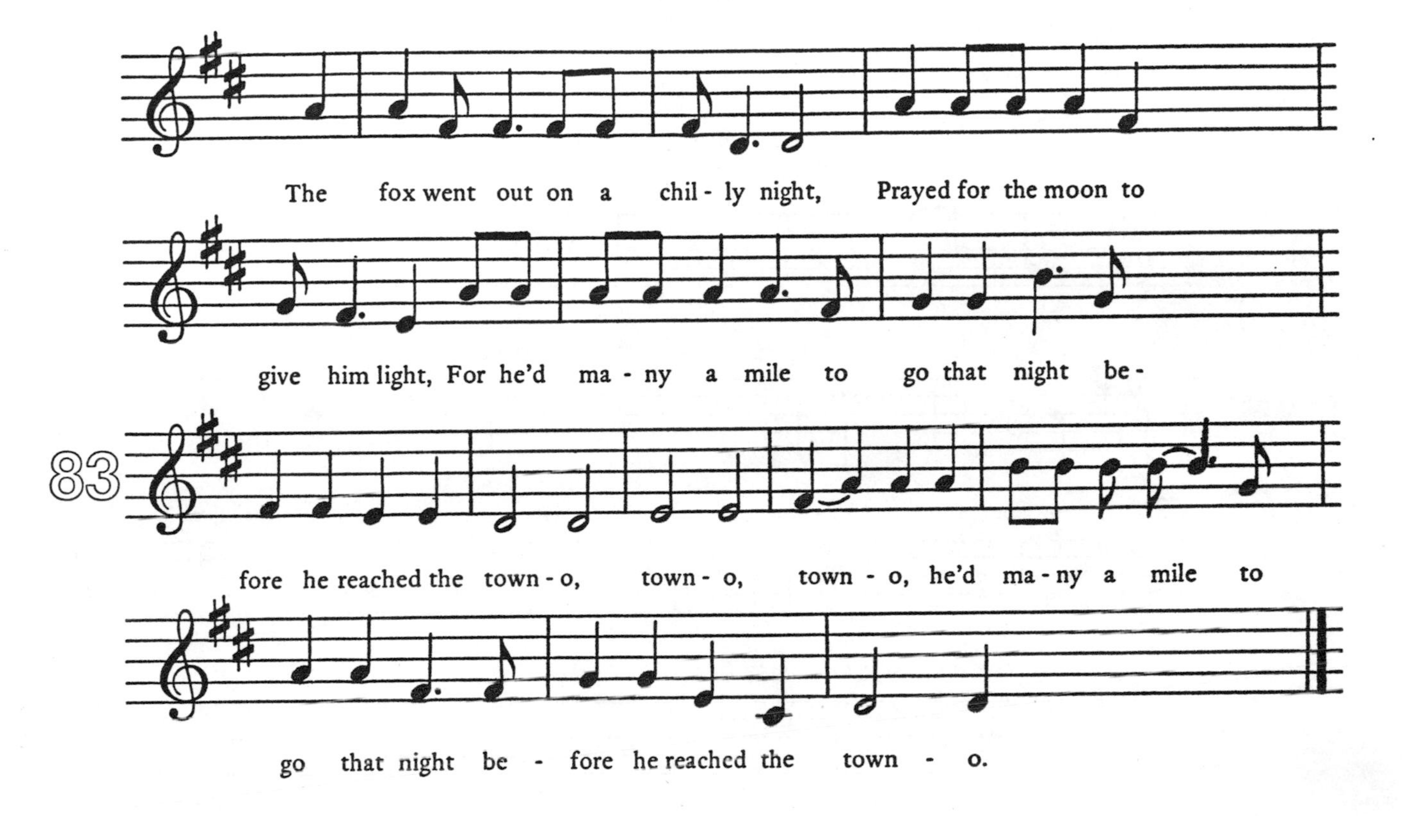

VERSES:

He ran till he came to a great big bin
The ducks and the geese were put therein,
Said, a couple of you will grease my chin
Before I leave this town-o, etc.

He grabbed the grey goose by the neck
Slung the little one over his back,
He didn't mind their quack-quack-quack
And the legs all dangling down-o, etc.

Old mother pitter-patter jumped out of bed
Out of the window she cocked her head
Crying, John, John, the grey goose is gone
And the fox is on the town-o, etc.

John, he went to the top of the hill
Blew his horn both loud and shrill;
The fox, he said, I better flee with my kill
He'll soon be on my trail-o, etc.

He ran till he came to his cozy den
There were the little ones, eight, nine, ten,
They said daddy, you better go back again,
'Cause it must be a mighty fine town-o, etc.

Then the fox and his wife without any strife
Cut up the goose with fork and knife,
They never had such a supper in their life
And the little ones chewed on the bones-o,
etc.

MY HORSES AIN'T HUNGRY

VERSES:

My parents don't like you, you're poor I am told,
But it's your love I'm wanting, not silver or gold.
Then come with me Polly, we'll ride till we come
To some little cabin, we'll call it our home.

Sparking is pleasure, but parting is grief,
And a false hearted lover is worse than a thief.
A thief will just rob you and take what you have,
But a false hearted lover will lead you to the grave.

A BEAR WENT OVER THE MOUNTAIN

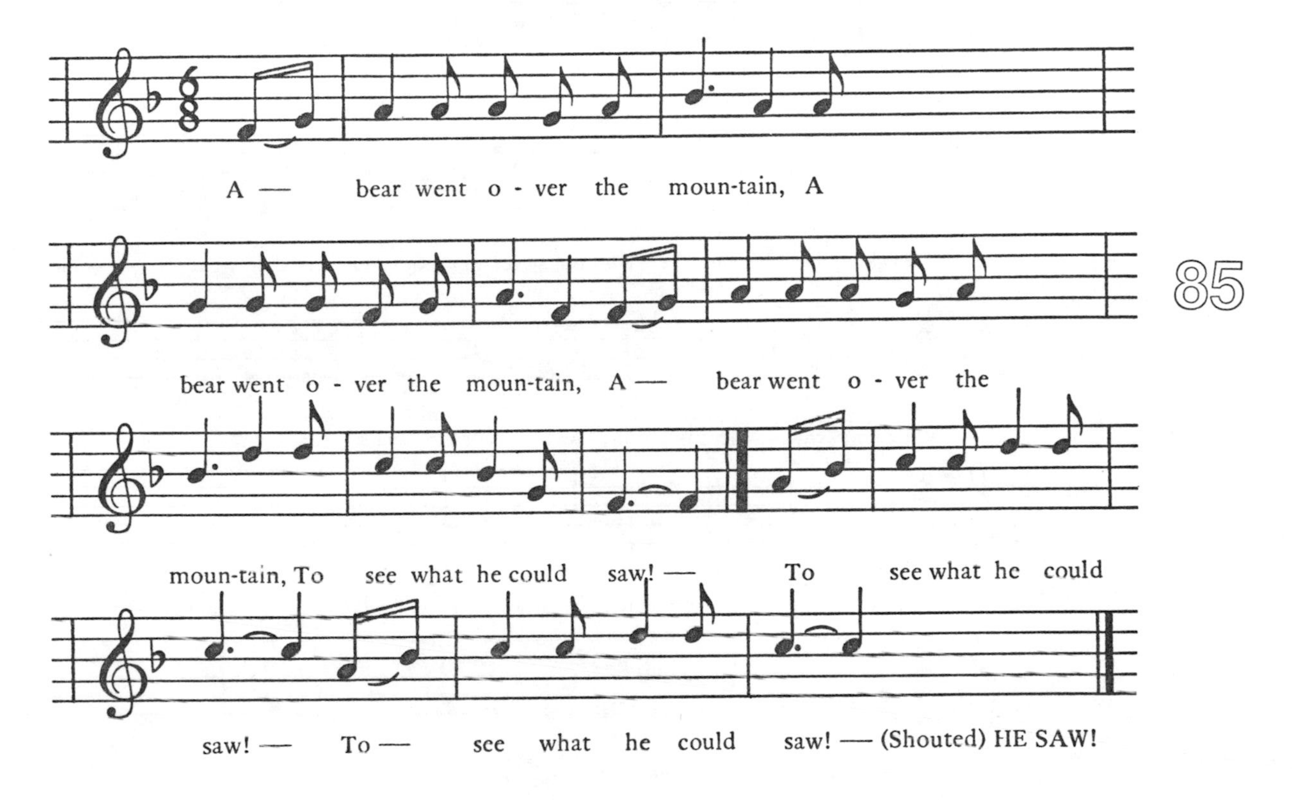

VERSES:

The other side of the mountain,
The other side of the mountain,
The other side of the mountain,
Was all what he could saw!
Was all what he could saw!
Was all what he could saw! (Shouted) OH!

WHEN I FIRST CAME TO THIS LAND

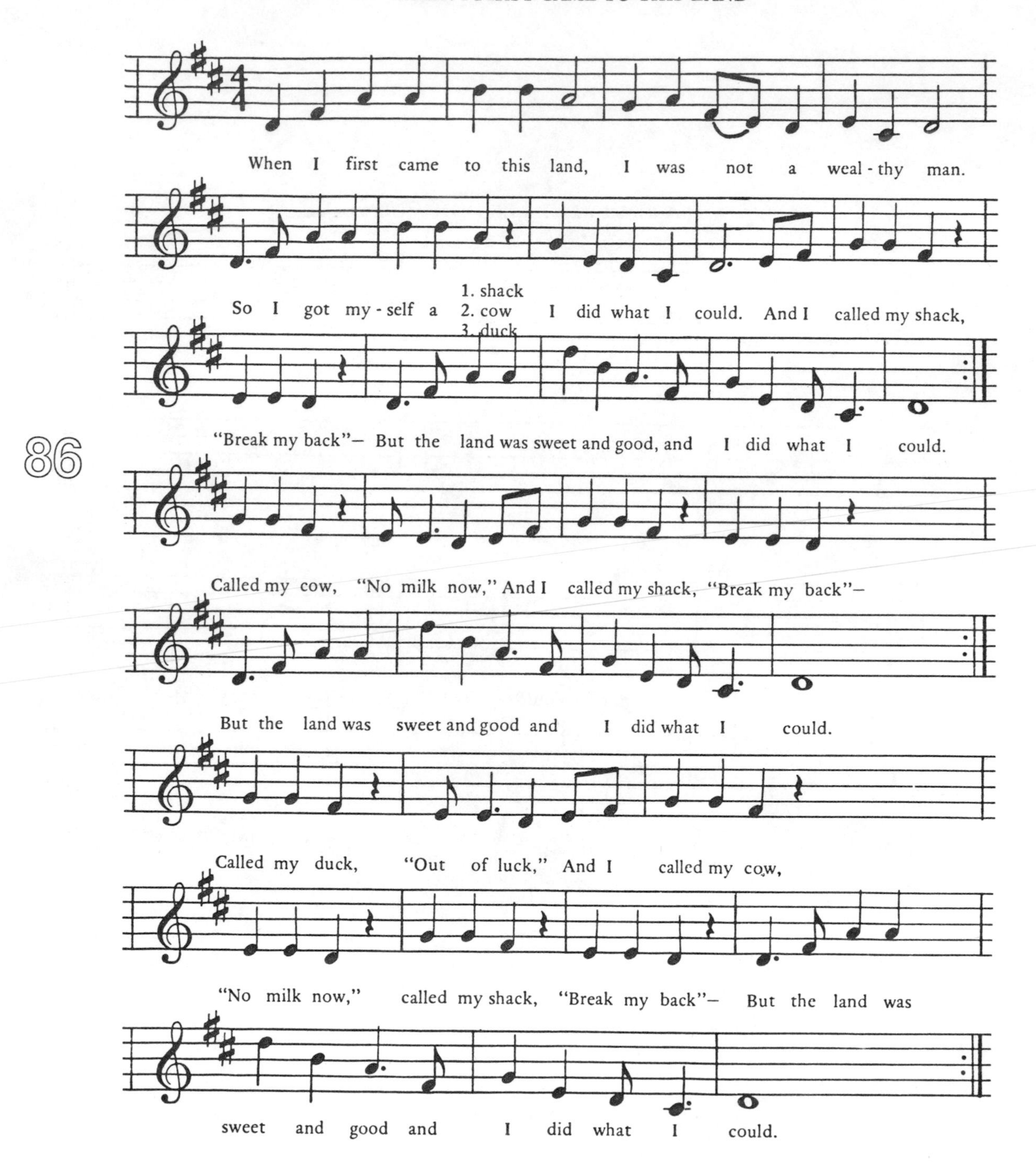

VERSES:
(Add verses 4 & 5 in a similar cumulative manner)

4th verse: Called my wife, run for your life.
5th verse: Called my son, my work's done.

BARBARA ALLEN

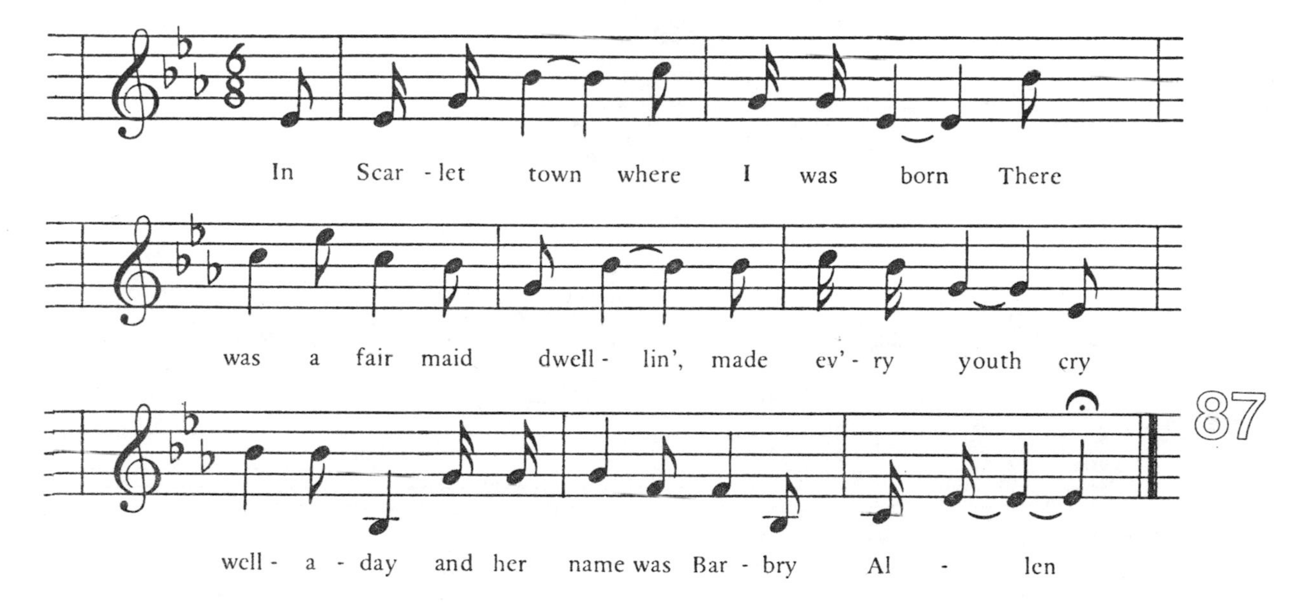

VERSES:

It was in the merry month of May
When green buds they were swelling;
Sweet William came from the west country
And he courted Barbara Allen.

He sent his servant unto her
To the place where she was dwelling;
Said my master's sick, bids me call for you
If your name be Barbara Allen.

Well, slowly, slowly got she up
And slowly went she nigh him;
But all she said as she passed his bed
Young man I think you're dying.

Then lightly tripped she down the stairs
She heard those church bells tolling;
And each bell seemed to say as it tolled
Hard-hearted Barbara Allen.

O, mother, mother go make my bed
And make it long and narrow;
Sweet William died for me today.
I'll die for him tomorrow.

They buried Barbara in the old church yard
They buried Sweet William beside her;
Out of his grave grew a red, red rose
And out of hers a briar.

They grew and grew up the old church wall,
Till they could grow no higher;
And at the top twined in a lover's knot
The red rose and the briar.

YANKEE DOODLE or FATHER AND I WENT DOWN TO CAMP

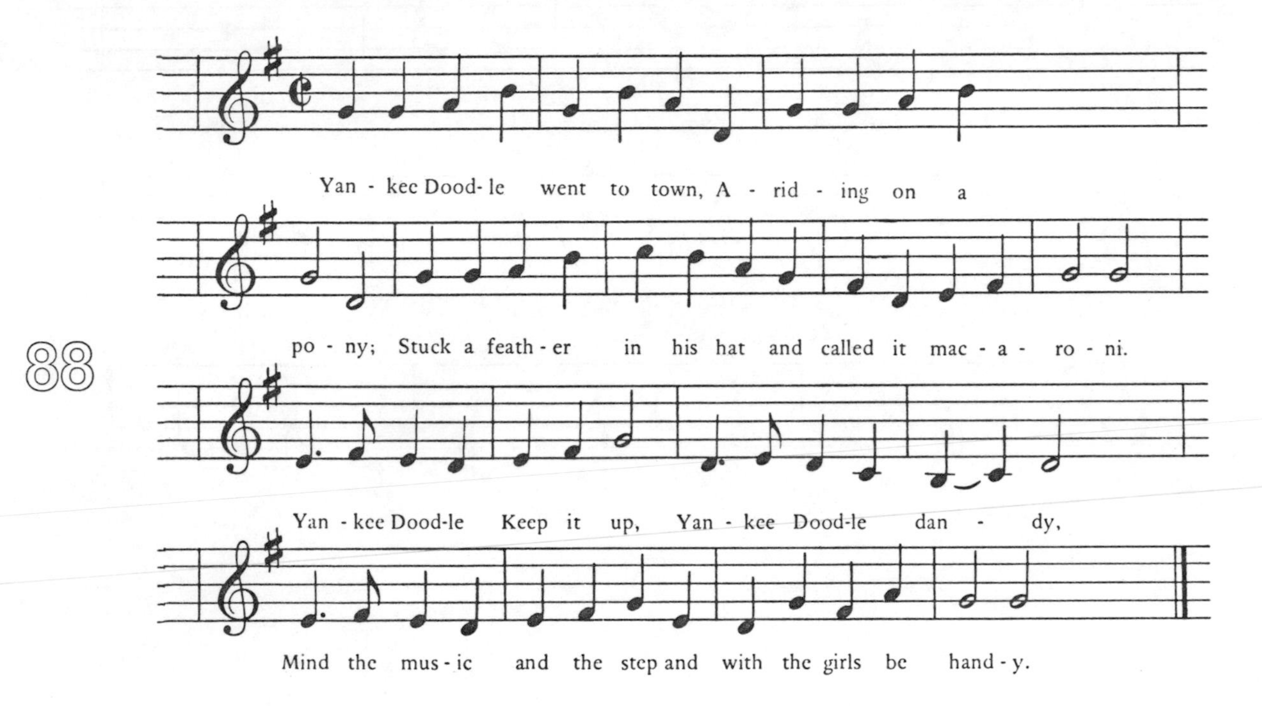

VERSES:

Father and I went down to camp
Along with Captain Gooding;
And there we saw the men and boys
As thick as hasty pudding.
(Chorus)

There was Captain Washington,
Upon a slapping stallion,
A-giving orders to his men,
I guess there was a million.
(Chorus)

And there we saw a thousand men,
As rich as 'Squire David,
And what they wasted every day,
I wish it could be sa-ved.
(Chorus)

And there I saw a pumpkin shell,
As big as mother's basin,
And every time they touched it off,
They scamper'd like the nation.
(Chorus)

LIBERTY SONG

This was the first popular hit song of America, written in 1768. Words by John Dickinson, music by William Boyce.

LIBERTY SONG (Continued)

CINDY

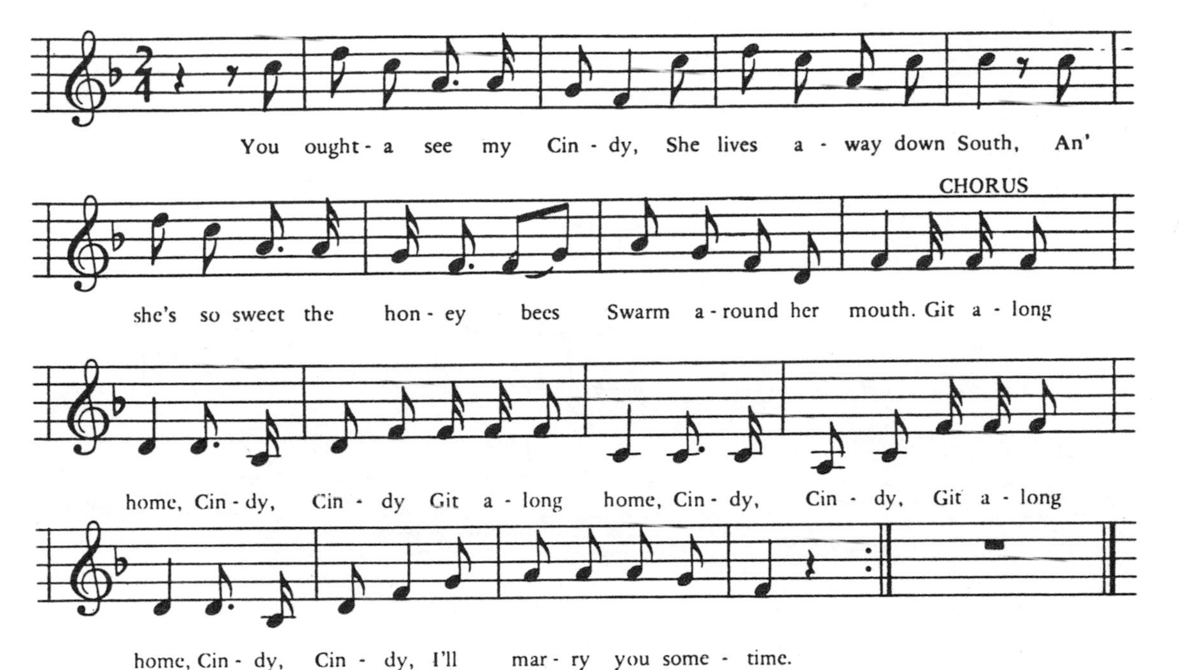

VERSES:

I wish I was an apple,
A-hangin' on a tree,
And everytime that pretty gal passed
She'd take a bite of me.
(Chorus)

I wish I had a needle,
As fine as I could sew,
I'd sew that gal to my coat tail
And down the road I'd go.
(Chorus)

When Cindy got religion
She thought her time had come,
She walked right up to the preacher
And chewed her chewin' gum.
(Chorus)

Cindy got religion,
She'd had it once before,
But when she heard my old banjo,
She 'uz the first un on the floor.
(Chorus)

She took me in her parlor,
She cooled me with her fan,
She swore that Ize the purties' thang
In the shape of mortal man.
(Chorus)

Cindy hugged and kissed me,
She wrung her hands and cried,
She swore I was the purties' thing
That ever lived or died.
(Chorus)

She told me that she loved me,
She called me sugar plum,
She throwed her arms around me
And I thought my time had come.
(Chorus)

HURRAH, LIE!

VERSES:

Seed the wood cut the axe, (2)
Seed the wood cut the axe, seed the chickens chewin' wax.
(Chorus)

Seed a eel eat a seal, (2)
Seed a hant climb the stairs, seed the badman sayin' his prayers.
(Chorus)

Seed a rat ketch a cat, (2)
Seed a rat ketch a cat—if you till a yarn that's bigger'n that.
(Chorus)

JOHNNY HAS GONE FOR A SOLDIER

VERSES:

Me O my, I loved him so,
Broke my heart to see him go,
And only time will heal my woe,
Johnny has gone for a soldier.

I'd sell my clock, I'd sell my reel,
Likewise I'd sell my spinning wheel
To buy my love a sword of steel–
Johnny has gone for a soldier.

DESE BONES GWINE RISE AGAIN

VERSES:

Thought he'd make a woman, too, Dese bones gwine rise again,
Didn't know 'xactly what to do, Dese bones gwine rise again.
(Chorus)

Took a rib from Adam's side, etc.
Made Miss Eve for to be his bride, etc.
(Chorus)

Put um in a gyarden fine and fair, etc.
Tole um to eat whatever was dere, etc.
(Chorus)

But to one tree they mus' not go, etc.
Must leave de apples dere to grow, etc.
(Chorus)

Sarpint quoiled around a chuck, etc.
At Miss Eve his eye he wunk, etc.
(Chorus)

First she took a little pull, etc.
Then she filled her apron full, etc.
(Chorus)

Adam took a little slice, etc.
Smack his lips an' say 'twas nice, etc.
(Chorus)

De Lord He spoke with a 'ponstrous voice, etc.
Shook de world to its very jois', etc.
(Chorus)

'Stole my apple, I believe,' etc.
'No, Marse Lord, I 'spec' it was Eve,' etc.
(Chorus)

'Out of this garden you must git, etc.
Earn yo' livin' by yo' sweat! etc.
(Chorus)

He put an angel at de do', etc.
Tol 'um never come dere no mo', etc.
(Chorus)

Of this tale there is no mo', etc.
Eve et the apple and Adam de co', etc.
(Chorus)

FELIX THE SOLDIER

VERSES:

But I couldn't beat the drum,
And I couldn't play the flute,
So they handed me a musket
And taught me how to shoot.

We had a bloody fight
After we had scaled the wall,
And the Divil a bit of mercy
Did the Frenchies have at all.

But the Injuns they were sly,
And the Frenchies, they were coy,
So they shot off the left leg
Of this poor Irish boy.

Then they put me on a ship,
And they sent me home again,
With all my army training
After battle's strife and din.

I will bid my spade adieu,
For I cannot dig the bog,
But I still can play a fiddle
And I still can drink my grog.

I have learned to smoke a pipe
And have learned to fire a gun,
To the Divil with the fighting,
I am glad the war is done.

OLD BANGUM

VERSES:

There is a wild boar in these woods
Dillum down dillum
There is a wild boar in these woods,
Dillum down
There is a wild boar in these woods,
Eats men's bones and drinks their blood.
Cubbi-kee, cuddledum, killi quo quam.

Old Bangum drew his wooden knife (3)
And swore he'd take the wild boar's life.
Old Bangum went to the wild boar's den (3)
And found the bones of a thousand men.
They fought four hours in that day (3)
The wild boar fled and slunk away.

Old Bangum, did you win or lose? (3)
He swore, by Jove, he'd won his shoes.

SAILING IN THE BOAT

VERSES:

Rose in the garden for you, young man (2)
Rose in the garden, get it if you can,
But take care not a frost-bitten one.
(Chorus)

Choose your partner, stay til day, (3)
And don't never mind what the old folks say.
(Chorus)

Old folks say 'tis the very best way (3)
To count all night and sleep all day.
(Chorus)

CHORUS:

Here she comes, so fresh and fair,
Sky-blue eyes and curly hair,
Rosy in cheek, dimple in her chin,
Say, young man, but you can't come in.

HOW OLD ARE YOU, MY PRETTY LITTLE MISS?

VERSES:

'Can you court, my pretty little miss?
Can you court, my flower?'
'I can court more in a minute and a half,
Than you can in an hour.'
(Chorus)

'Will you marry me, my pretty little miss?
Will you marry me, good looking?'
'I'll marry you, but I won't do
Your washing or your cooking!'
(Chorus)

CHORUS:

Sink to my dink to my diddle diddle dum,
Rink to my dink to my doodle (Repeat)

RATTLESNAKE

VERSES:

Muskrat, O muskrat,
What makes you smell so bad?
I've been in the bottom all of my life
Till I'm mortified in my head, head, etc.

Groundhog, groundhog,
What makes your back so brown?
It's a wonder I don't smotherfy,
Livin' down in the ground, ground, etc.

Rooster, O rooster,
What makes your claws so hard?
Been scratchin' this gravel all my days.
It's a wonder I ain't tired, etc.

Jaybird, O jaybird,
What makes you fly so high?
Been robbin' your cornpatch all my life,
It's a wonder I don't die, die, etc.

THE GOLDEN VANITY

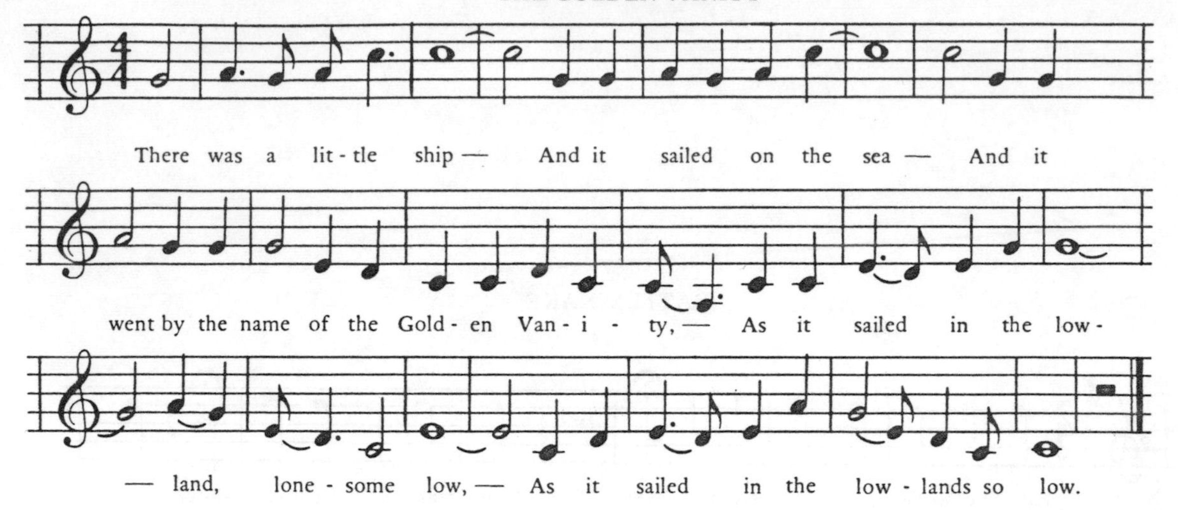

VERSES:

There was another ship
That sailed upon the sea,
And the name that they called her
Was the Turkey Roveree,

CHORUS:

As it sailed in the lowland, lonesome low
As it sailed in the lowlands so low.

Captain, O Captain
Now what will you give me,
If I will sink
That Turkey Roveree?
As she sails, etc.

O I will give you gold
And I will give you fee,
And my fairest daughter
Will be wed to thee,
If you sink her in the, etc.

So he bowed his breast
And away swum he,
And he swum till he come
To the Turkey Roveree,
As she rolled in the, etc.

Some was playin' cards
And some was playin' dice,
And some was taking,
Their best friends' advice,
As she rolled in the, etc.

He had a little instrument
Just fitted for his use,
And he bored nine holes
And he bored them all at once,
And he sank her in the, etc.

Some threw their hats
And some threw their caps,
They all tried to stop
Them awful water gaps,
As she sunk in the, etc.

Well, he bowed to his breast
And back swum he,
He swum till he come
To the Golden Vanity,
As she rolled in the, etc.

Captain, O Captain
Take me on board,
And do unto me
As good as your word,
For I'm drowning in the, etc.

But he hoisted his sails
And away sailed he,
And he left that poor sailor boy
To drown in the sea,
To drown in the lowland, lonesome low,
To drown in the lonesome sea.

THE RIDDLE

This song appeared in the colonies around the middle of the 18th Century. Pioneer children enjoyed all kinds of games and riddles to pass the time away on their long trek West. This was a riddle they could sing, and thus it became one of their favorites.

THE RIDDLE SONG

VERSES:

How can there be a cherry that has no stone?
How can there be a chicken that has no bone?
How can there be a ring that has no end?
How can there be a baby with no cryin'?

A cherry when it's bloomin' it has no stone,
A chicken in an eggshell it has no bone,
A ring when it is rollin' it has no end,
A baby when it's sleepin' has no cryin'.

THERE WAS A TREE STOOD IN THE GROUND

This song was fun for colonial children. It may be sung in unison. Verses may be divided by groups.

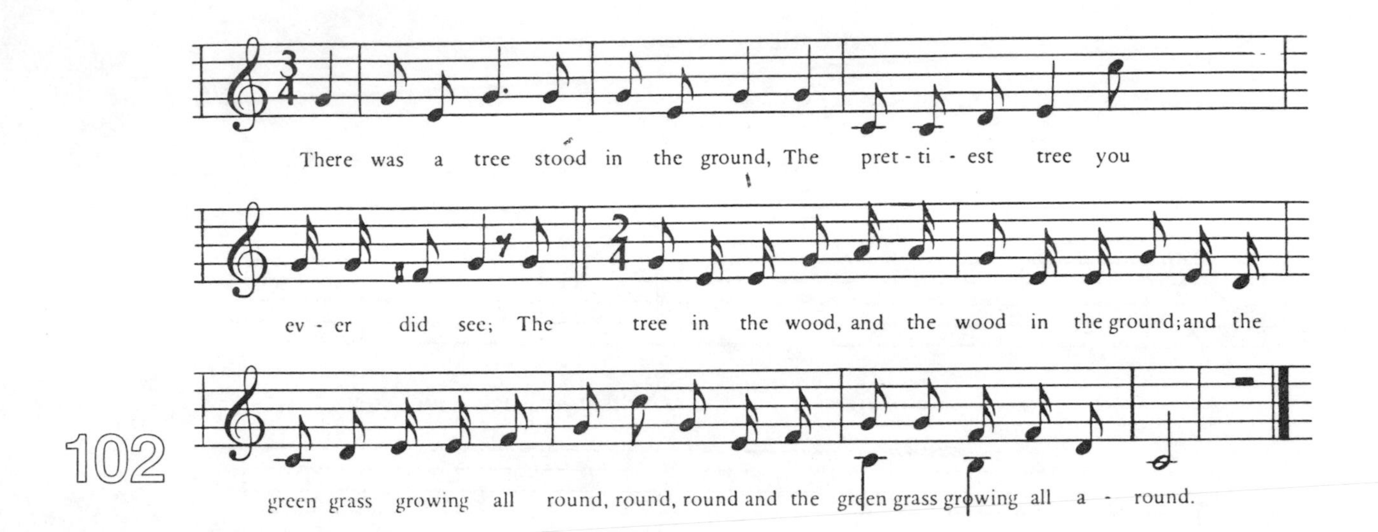

VERSES:

And on this tree there was a limb,
The prettiest limb you ever did see;
The limb on the tree, and the tree in the wood,
The tree in the wood, and the wood in the ground,
And the green grass growing all round, round, round
And the green grass growing all around.

And on the limb there was a bough,
The prettiest bough you ever did see;
The bough on the limb, and the limb on the tree, etc.

And on this bough there was a twig,
The prettiest twig you ever did see;
The twig on the bough, and the bough on the limb, etc.

And on the twig there was a nest, etc.
And in this nest there were some eggs, etc.
And in the eggs there was a bird, etc.
And on the bird there was a wing, etc.
And on the wing there was a feather, etc.
And on the feather there was some down,
The prettiest down you ever did see;
The down on the feather, and the feather on the wing,
The feather on the wing, and the wing on the bird,
The wing on the bird, and the bird in the eggs,
The bird in the eggs, and the eggs in the nest
The eggs in the nest, and the nest on the twig
The twig on the bough, and the bough on the limb,
The bough on the limb, and the limb on the tree
The limb on the tree, and the tree in the wood,
The tree in the wood, and the wood in the ground,
And the green grass growing all round, round, round,
And the green grass growing all round.

THE GIRL I LEFT BEHIND ME

"The Girl I Left Behind Me" was brought to America by English and Irish immigrants. This song has been associated with Archibald Willard's painting, "Spirit of '76." For many years West Point has used this number as a march when the graduating class assembles for the last time in June.

103

VERSES:

For she is as fair as Shannon's side
And so much purer than its water
But she did refuse to be my bride
Though many years I had sought her.

Then to France I went and sailed away
Her letters oft remind me
That I promised never to gain-say
The girl I left behind me.

Now she says "My own dear love come home
My friends are rich and they are many
Or abroad with you I want to roam
A soldier's heart stout as any.

But if you'll not come nor let me go
I'll think you have resigned me."
Oh my heart nigh broke when I said "no"
To the girl I left behind me.

Never shall my only true love brave
A life of war and heavy toiling,
Never never as a skulking slave
I'll tread my own native soil on.

But if it were free or to be freed,
The battle's close would find me
To my Ireland bound, nor message need
From the girl I left behind me.

A FROG WENT A-COURTING

Migrating New Englanders brought this song with them to their new homes in the Southern Appalachians, and it became a popular children's song. During the period of national expansion this song spread over the entire country, and today there are hundreds of versions and verses. It may be sung in groups, acting out verses.

VERSES:

He rode till he reached Miss Mouse's door, aha, ho, ho,
He rode till he reached Miss Mouse's door,
Where he had often been before, aha, ho, ho.

He sat little mousie on his knee, aha, ho, ho, etc.
And said "Miss Mousie, marry me," aha, ho, ho.

She said "I will ask my Uncle Rat," aha, ho, ho, etc.
"And see what he will say to that", aha, ho, ho.

Hence old Uncle Rat did ride to town, aha, ho, ho, etc.
To buy his niece a wedding gown, aha, ho, ho.

Now where will the wedding supper be, aha, ho, ho, etc.
Down Yonder in the hollow tree, aha, ho, ho.

The first to arrive was big brown bug, aha, ho, ho, etc.
He drowned in the molasses jug, aha, ho, ho.

The next to arrive was Parson Fly, aha, ho, ho, etc.
He ate so much he nearly died, aha, ho, ho.

The next to arrive was big Tom cat, aha, ho, ho, etc.
He chased Miss Mouse and Uncle Rat, aha, ho, ho.

The last to arrive was Dick the Drake, aha, ho, ho, etc.
Who chased the frog into the lake, aha, ho, ho.

Now go put the songbook on the shelf, aha, ho, ho
Now go put the songbook on the shelf.
If you want more go sing yourself, aha, ho, ho.

SKIP TO MY LOU

CHORUS: (to be sung when you feel like it):
Lou, Lou, skip to my Lou. (3)
Skip to my Lou, my darlin'.

VERSES:
Lost my partner, what'll I do? (3)
Skip to my Lou, my darlin'.

I'll get another one, purtier'n you, (3)
Skip to my Lou, my darlin'

Can't get a red bird, a blue bird'll do, (3)
Skip to my Lou, my darlin'.

Little red wagon, painted blue.
Fly in the sugar-bowl, shoo, fly, shoo.
Gone again, what'll I do?
Hair in the butterdish, six feet long.
Cows in the cornfield, two by two.
Rats in the breadtray, how they chew.
One old boat and a run-down shoe.
Cats in the buttermilk.
Needle in the haystack, two by two.
Pickles are sour and so are you.
Pa's got a shot gun, number 32.
Hurry up slow poke, do oh, do.
Mules in the cellar, kicking up through.
Dad's old hat got torn in two.
My girl wears a number nine shoe.
Pretty as a red bird, prettier too.
Sugar is sweet and so are you.
When I go a courtin' I take two.
I've got another one sweeter than you.
Had a little cart and a pony too.
He's got big feet and awkward too.
If you don't have a necktie a shoestring will do.
Bears in the rosebush, boo, boo, boo.
Kitten in the haymow, mew, mew, mew.
We'll keep it up until half past two.

106

11 Make Your Own Musical Instruments

CONTRARY TO POPULAR BELIEF, the Puritans did permit music and developed a reputation for making fine musical instruments.

The first pipe organ did not arrive in the colonies until 1700, when it was installed in the Episcopal Church at Port Royal, Virginia. The first pipe organ built in the colonies was manufactured in 1737 and placed in Trinity Church, New York City. The first American-made piano is believed to have been manufactured in 1776 by John Behrent in Philadelphia.

The following incident indicates the strangeness and power of musical instruments in the New World. In 1741 Indians prepared to attack a Moravian settlement in Bethlehem, Pennsylvania. They fled when they heard the sound of the Moravian native instrument, the trombone.

You can make the following musical instruments, to get more of a feeling for what music sounded like two centuries ago.

THE GLASSYCHORD

The "glassychord," or harmonica, was invented by Benjamin Franklin. It consisted of a series of glass discs which were turned by a foot pedal. The discs were partially immersed in water and mounted on a table; they produced a sound like a spoon gently tapping a half-filled glass of water.

To approximate a glassychord, fill glasses with water at different levels and create a scale by changing the water levels and tapping the glasses gently with a spoon. The lower the water level the higher the note. See how many tunes you can play on the glasses.

RINGING GLASSES

Another colonial way of producing music was by ringing glasses. A lovely tone can be produced by moistening a finger and pressing gently on the rim while moving the finger around the circumference. About one revolution per second produces a good sound. Different tones result from different types of glass and the level of fluid in each.

Tear drop or tulip glasses usually produce the best tones, as does thin glass and crystal.

THE COLONIAL MARCHING DRUM

The colonial marching drum symbolizes the Revolution as few instruments do. The drum roll was used to call the troops to order, to give field commands, and to mark cadences. Drums were made entirely from wood and animal skins. The drums produced a deep heavy sound and were generally played at a cadence of more than twenty steps per minute, slower than today.

Drums can be made from nearly any cylindrical object (e.g., old cans, oatmeal boxes, or empty tobacco canisters). Tin cans and metal objects can leave sharp edges; make sure the edges are filed down or taped so no one gets cut.

COFFEE CAN DRUM

An old coffee can with a plastic top makes an excellent drum. Two pencils with erasers are good drumsticks. Besides the plastic lids, other good drumhead materials include cut up inner tubes, oilcloth, surgical rubber, material (cotton), and animal hides. Coffee cans can be decorated by painting them red, white, and blue, adding imitation cords, or placing decals of eagles and flags on them.

MIXING BOWL KETTLE DRUM

The kettle drum was also popular in colonial times. If you are fortunate enough to find an old wooden mixing bowl, you can construct an interesting replica. Simply stretch the drumhead material over the bowl to make sure it fits. Then place one tack through the material into the bowl. Now put a tack in the opposite side, while drawing the material tight. Move to the sides and repeat the procedure, until there are enough tacks to insure the drumhead will not sag.

FIFE

The fife, an instrument very similar to the flute or piccolo, is generally associated with colonial drum corps. It is very small in circumference and only about a foot long. The fife is held horizontal to the ground with the fingers of both hands used to cover six holes. A hole near one end of the fife faces up while the body of the instrument is held against the lower lip. By gently blowing into this hole and lifting fingers individually or in combinations, different tones are produced. The fife is an octave above the flute and produces a high shrill sound; it differs from the piccolo in that it has holes instead of keys.

Though it is not widely known, the fife was also used by our Southern agrarian culture to provide music for dances, singing, and other festive occasions. Negro servants often made fifes from sugar cane stalks, willow branches, or tree bark. Colonial Williamsburg in Virginia maintains the tradition by having their Fife and Drum Corps play in the commons of the town at certain times during the year.

A fife can be imitated with a cola bottle. Place the opening of the bottle against the lower lip and gently blow across the top, until you make a pleasing sound. Filling bottles with water at different levels produces different sounds. A group can make a scale and then play a song, with each child playing *his note* at the appropriate time. "Yankee Doodle" is a dandy song for this.

WILLOW WHISTLE

With a willow branch and a knife, you can make a willow whistle. Take a small branch from a weeping willow and cut off a 5- or 6-inch section. At one end smooth a spot for your lips. About 2 inches from that end carve a small notch. Next soak the bark and slide it off. Cut a groove (split) from the notch to the mouthpiece. Now slide the bark back on and blow. Keep the whistle wet and recut the notches if necessary.

IMPROVISED INSTRUMENTS

During the revolutionary period people could not afford elaborate instruments and often did not have time to build them. This did not lessen their desire to make music, so there evolved a unique set of instruments that ranged from the jaw bone of a horse to hambone (slapping one's own body). Little is known about where various homemade instruments originated, or at what time in history they began to be used. Written information on improvised instruments is limited, and the imagination can run wild and consider almost anything that makes a sound.

Playing improvised instruments is an especially good activity for young children; it costs nothing and requires no instruction. The following are some simple homemade improvised instruments that may well have been used in the late 18th century.

TRIANGLES
A triangle can be made by bending in a vise any piece of metal that has a resonant quality. Simply bend in two places to form a triangle, suspend from a string, and tap rhythmically with another piece of metal. One triangle could consist of a metal horseshoe suspended from a string and tapped with a piece of metal.

POTS AND PANS
Stuff some old rags in different sized pots and pans. Arrange them on the floor from high sounds to low sounds and experiment by tapping on them with different objects (e.g., wooden spoons, metal spoons, pencils with erasers).

SPOONS
Playing the spoons has traditionally turned into an art form. There are but a few good spoon players in America today. Recently spoons have been used on popular Bluegrass recordings.

Spoons are played by placing the stems between the first and third fingers with the bowl bottoms toward each other. The spoons are then slapped in the hand, or more commonly between the hand and thigh. This produces a unique clicking sound.

JUGS
Perhaps the first man to ever play a jug had first consumed the contents thereof. The jug is played by holding the opening close to the lips and half blowing and half spitting into it. The resulting sound is a low, airy, bellowing, belching noise. Any glass cider jug will do but crock or earthenware jugs give the best tone. The bigger the jug the better.

COMB AND WAX PAPER
Place a clean comb to the lips. On the opposite side hold a piece of wax paper taut. Breathe out and hum to produce a sound just like a kazoo.

WASHBOARDS
It is a known fact that when frontier women were not doing the wash, frontier men were playing the washboards. All you need to do is find a washboard and run a stick or spoon over the rippled surface in time with the music.

SHAKERS
Shakers (maracas) can be made of almost anything, including a balloon filled with paper clips (though the colonists didn't have paper clips and balloons, they surely had gourds and stones). Another possibility is to fill a pop-top can with rice or dried peas and tape the hole. Decorate the can any way you want; it has a great sound.

BULL ROARER
This is a thin wood slat about 2 inches wide and 12 inches long. Cut the bull roarer as shown in the illustration, and sand it smooth. Twirl overhead at the end of a long string to produce a deep whirring sound. This is an old mountain toy as well as an instrument.

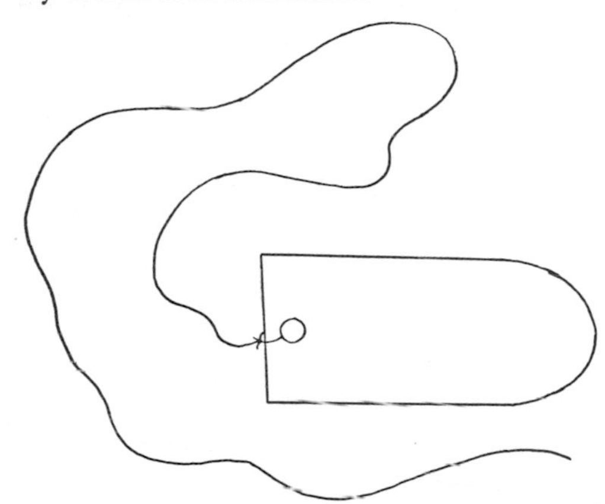

WISHBONE HARP
Save a wishbone from the dinner chicken or turkey. String a small thin rubber band across the opening. Wind the rubber band to change the tone. Put the end of the wishbone harp on a table or empty can to improve the sound.

SLINGSHOT STRUMMER

Find a Y-shaped branch. Put in three screws for pegs along one prong; stretch three rubber bands across. Use bands of the same size; arrange them so that each one is tighter than the one below it.

SHOEBOX STRUMMER

Remove the cover from a cardboard cigar or shoe box; use only the open box. Cut small grooves half an inch from both ends of the shorter sides with an ordinary kitchen knife. Select a thin, short rubber band, and string it around the box, fitting it into the pair of grooves nearest you. Then put the widest, longest band into the grooves on the far end. Measure off two more pairs of grooves an equal distance between the two end grooves. String two more rubber bands, grading them as to size. Pluck the strummer with your fingers or a used kitchen match.

BOX BANJO

Find a sturdy, small carton (cereal, dry milk, or whipped butter).

One inch from the edge, cut out a semicircular sound hole. Then cut a 1-inch slit an inch below the first hole.

To make the bridge, cut a 2-inch square of heavy cardboard. From two corners remove 1/2-inch squares so the bridge has a one-inch tab.

Fit the bridge into the slit, and string the banjo with four rubber bands of different sizes. The smaller ones will stretch more and produce the higher notes. Pluck the rubber bands gently with your fingers or with a used kitchen match.

Ceremonial Gatherings

Here are a collection of ideas for special events, colonial-type get togethers for the family, neighborhood or community. Other gatherings can provide information about our flag, its history, ceremonies and traditions. What a wonderful way to celebrate our country's birthday honoring our heritage!

112

12 Special Events: Bees, Bonfires and Colonial Fairs

SPECIAL EVENTS CAN ADD ADDITIONAL SPARKLE to group programs, or culminate activities for schools, recreation centers, camps, or other groups. Special events are attention-getters, they are great fun as social occasions, and they help create an environment . . . like it was.

There is no substitute for thorough, careful planning with participants. What do *they* want to do? Is the activity feasible? What committees and/or organization are needed? How much money is needed? What supplies are required? What about transportation, promotion timetables, etc.? A leader can help; assist, guide—but finally the participants themselves make or break the undertaking. Here are some suggested activities to whet your appetite.

BEES

In colonial times men and women gathered to help one another accomplish some major task. This was called a "bee" and it was also an opportunity to catch up on the latest gossip.

The colonists gathered for many reasons: candlemaking, soapmaking, gathering maple sap, spinning, weaving, "putting down" great quantities of preserves, cornhusking, planting crops, mending fences, repairing town buildings or roads, spring cleaning, cutting and storing hay, gathering rushes, gathering crops, banking homes, rolling logs, pulling stumps, clearing rocks, house and barn raisings, apple paring, sewing, and quiltmaking.

Remember the philosophy of the colonists—it is easier to do anything with a group than individually. Keep in mind the possibilities for service projects as you look over these adaptations of bees.

SEWING OR QUILTING BEE

These can be used to teach basic sewing skills or employ more advanced skills. Making stuffed animals for hospitals, doll's clothes for children who don't have them, or lap robes for wheelchair patients are possibilities. Such items as pot holders, dishcloths, pincushions, and aprons can be sold at charity bazaars. Projects can be set up on an assembly-line basis with different people doing different parts of the work.

CORN HUSKING BEE

This is suitable for rural or near-rural areas. Have teams race to see which can husk a bushel of corn fastest and award prizes (or give prizes to anyone who finds a red ear first). Then sell the corn or give it to a public service group. It can also be roasted or baked in a pit fire and eaten. Colorful ears may be set aside as Thanksgiving decorations.

SPELLING BEE

This is a common game used in classrooms now as it was 200 years ago. Lists of words are drawn up in advance. Two teams are seated in opposite lines and the team to go first is chosen by a flip of a coin. If the first person spells the first word right he scores a point for his team and moves to the end of the line. If he misses, the first person on the opposing team gets to try the word; if he misses also the word is not used again. This proceeds until all members have had a chance. The team scoring the most points wins.

GREASED WATERMELON BATTLE AND FEAST

AGE GROUP: 12-14 or 14-16
PARTICIPANTS: 6-8 per team
MATERIALS: Watermelon; lard or vegetable shortening; swimming pool
DIRECTIONS: This works best in a swimming pool, with water at roughly a 3-foot depth. It is a rather rough activity and should be carefully supervised. Teams should be as evenly matched as possible. At a signal, each team goes toward the watermelon, which has been generously greased. This is similar to catching a greased pig—but perhaps more humane! The team succeeding in getting the watermelon to a predetermined goal or over a specified line wins. After the contest a watermelon feast ensues.

ILLUMINATION BONFIRES

Bonfires were built in the streets in colonial times, and many windows had candles in them as part of the occasion. Bonfires were lit to celebrate such events as the surrender of Cornwallis on October 19, 1781. Have one to celebrate a holiday, such as the Fourth of July—but first secure proper permission(s) and observe safety precautions.

BICENTENNIAL FAIRS

Colonial fairs featured such activities as foot races, wrestling, bouts at cudgels, catching a greased pig, and climbing a greased pole. These could be duplicated or adapted. A Bicentennial fair could also feature a bake sale, jams and jellies, ice cream, and other foods, perhaps using historical recipes. An exhibit of embroidery made using colonial techniques would be interesting as would homemade candles, baskets, jewelry, etc.

Other possibilities are Fourth-of-July picnics, Indian pageants, and other celebrations of patriotic events in American history. If you live near the sites of historic events or battles, be sure and capitalize on them in your program.

13 Flag Ceremonies

HISTORY OF THE FLAG, THE ANTHEM AND THE PLEDGE OF ALLEGIANCE

FLAGS HAVE LONG BEEN USED RITUALISTICALLY to symbolize countries, states, cities and organizations. The United States of America is no exception. It took less than one year from the birth of our nation on July 4, 1776, for the Continental Congress to authorize our flag. When the first American flag was authorized on June 14, 1777 it was known as the "Stars and Stripes." It had 13 stars, one for each of the thirteen original colonies. Since then, the flag has undergone considerable growth—it now has 50 stars, for the 50 states we now have.

The forty-eight star flag which President Taft created was our national emblem for forty-six years. Not until January 3, 1959, when Alaska was admitted to the Union, was the flag changed. Within a few months it was changed again when Hawaii became the fiftieth state. This called for a new design for the flag, which President Eisenhower described in Executive Order No. 10834, issued August 21, 1959.

Included in that Executive Order were the official dimensions of flags. The largest official flag is 20 feet wide and 38 feet long, while the smallest is one and 32/100 feet wide and 2-1/2 feet long.

The U.S. Flag is the only national flag in the world that is also the subject of the national anthem. "The Star Spangled Banner" was written by Francis Scott Key about the second official Stars and Stripes as it flew over Fort McHenry during the War of 1812.

The United States also has a pledge by which Americans swear their allegiance to their flag and country: "I pledge allegiance to the flag of the United States of America and to the Republic for which it stands, one Nation under God, indivisible, with liberty and justice for all." This present wording is not the only flag pledge that has been used over the years. The first pledge reads: "I give my hand and heart to my country, one nation, one language, one flag." A newspaper man, James B. Upham, decided in 1890 that patriotism was dying out, and felt that a new, more stirring pledge would help create a new wave of patriotism. He started a campaign to get school children to buy American flags to fly over their school, and it was a great success. The end of his campaign was to invent a pledge for the flag, which was to be introduced on the four hundredth anniversary of Columbus Day in 1892. With the help of a co-worker, Francis Bellamy, the new pledge was written. At that time, it read, "I pledge allegiance to my flag and to the Republic for which it stands—one Nation indivisible, with liberty and justice for all." Upham and Bellamy's pledge was amended when the National Flag Conference in 1923-24 replaced the phrase "my flag" with "flag of the United States of America," and when Congress added the phrase "under God" in 1954.

FLAG CODE AND TRADITION

The United States has specific laws and regulations governing the display and use of its flag. These regulations are found in Public Law No. 829, which follows in its entirety.

Public Law 829-77th Congress
Chapter 806-2d Session
H. J. Res. 359
Joint Resolution

To amend Public Law Numbered 623, approved June 22, 1942, entitled "Joint resolution to codify and emphasize existing rules and customs pertaining to the display and use of the flag of the United States of America."

Resolved by the Senate and House of Representatives of the United States of America in Congress Assembled, that Public Law Number 623, approved June 22, 1942 entitled "Joint resolution to codify and emphasize existing rules and customs pertaining to the display and use of the flag of the United States of America," be, and the same is hereby amended to read as follows:

That the following codification of existing rules and customs pertaining to the display and use of the flag of the United States of America be, and it is hereby, established for the use of such civilians or civilian groups or organizations as may not be required to conform with regulations promulgated by one or more executive departments of the Government of the United States.

Sec. 2. (a) It is the universal custom to display the flag only from sunrise to sunset on buildings and on stationary flagstaffs in the open. However, the flag may be displayed at night upon special occasions when it is desired to produce a patriotic effect.

(b) The flag should be hoisted briskly and lowered ceremoniously.

(c) The flag should not be displayed on days when the weather is inclement.

(d) The flag should be displayed on all days when the weather permits, especially on New Year's Day, January 1; Inauguration Day, January 20; Lincoln's Birthday, February 12; Washington's Birthday, February 22; Army Day, April 6; Easter Sunday (variable); Mother's Day, second Sunday in May; Memorial Day (half staff until noon), May 30; Flag Day, June 14; Independence Day, July 4; Labor Day, first Monday in September; Constitution Day, September 17; Columbus Day, October 12; Navy Day, October 27; Armistice Day, November 11; Thanksgiving Day, fourth Thursday in November; Christmas Day, December 25; such other days as may be proclaimed by the President of the United States; the birthdays of States (dates of admission); and on State holidays.

(e) The flag should be displayed daily, weather permitting, on or near the main administration building of every public institution.

(f) The flag should be displayed in or near every polling place on election days.

(g) The flag should be displayed during school days in or near every schoolhouse.

Sec. 3 That the flag, when carried in a procession with another flag or flags, should be either on the marching right; that is, the flag's own right, or, if there is a line of other flags, in front of the center of that line.

(a) The flag should not be displayed on a float in a parade except from a staff, or as provided in subsection (i).

(b) The flag should not be draped over the hood, top, sides or back of a vehicle or of a railroad train or a boat. When the flag is displayed on a motor car, the staff shall be fixed firmly to the chassis or clamped to the radiator cap.

(c) No other flag or pennant should be placed above or, if on the same level, to the right of the flag of the United States of America, except during church services conducted by naval chaplains at sea, when the church pennant may be flown above the flag during church services for the personnel of the Navy.

(d) The flag of the United States of America, when it is displayed with another flag against a wall from crossed staffs, should be on the right, the flag's own right, and its staff should be in front of the staff of the other flag.

(e) The flag of the United States of America should be at the center and at the highest point of the group when a number of flags of States or localities or pennants of societies are grouped and displayed from staffs.

(f) When flags of States, cities, or localities, or pennants of societies are flown on the same halyard with the flag of the United States, the latter should always be at the peak. When the flags are flown from adjacent staffs, the flag of the United States should be hoisted first and lowered last. No such flag or pennant may be placed above the flag of the United States or to the right of the flag of the United States.

(g) When flags of two or more nations are displayed, they are to be flown from separate staffs of the same height. The flags should be of approximately equal size. International usage forbids the display of the flag of one nation above that of another nation in time of peace.

(h) When the flag of the United States is [illegible]ed from a staff projecting horizontally or at an angle from the window sill, balcony, or front of a building, the union of the flag should be placed at the peak of the staff unless the flag is at half staff. When the flag is suspended over a sidewalk from a rope extending from a house to a pole at the edge of the sidewalk, the flag should be hoisted out, union first, from the building.

(i) When the flag is displayed otherwise than by being flown from a staff, it should be displayed flat, whether indoors or out, or so suspended that its folds fall as free as though the flag were staffed.

(j) When the flag is displayed over the middle of the street, it should be suspended vertically with the union to the north in an east and west street or to the east in a north and south street.

(k) When used on a speaker's platform, the flag, if displayed flat, should be displayed above and behind the speaker. When displayed from a staff in a church or public auditorium, if it is displayed in the chancel of a church, or on the speaker's platform in a public auditorium, the flag should occupy the position of honor and be placed at the clergyman's or speaker's right as he faces the congregation or audience. Any other flag so displayed in the chancel or on the platform should be placed at the clergyman's or speaker's left as he faces the congregation or audience. But when the flag is displayed from a staff in a church or public auditorium elsewhere than in the chancel or on the platform it shall be placed in the position of honor at the right of the congregation or audience as they face the chancel or platform. Any other flag so displayed should be placed on the left of the congregation or audience as they face the chancel or platform.

(1) The flag should form a distinctive feature of the ceremony of unveiling a statue or monument, but it should never be used as the covering for the statue or monument.

(m) The flag, when flown at half staff, should be first hoisted to the peak for an instant and then lowered to the half-staff position. The flag should be again raised to the peak before it is lowered for the day. By "half staff" is meant lowering the flag to one-half the distance between the top and bottom of the staff. Crepe streamers may be affixed to spear heads or flagstaffs in a parade only by order of the President of the United States.

(n) When the flag is used to cover a casket, it should be so placed that the union is at the head and over the left shoulder. The flag should not be lowered into the grave or allowed to touch the ground.

Sec. 4. That no disrespect should be shown to the flag of the United States of America; the flag should not be dipped to any person or thing. Regimental colors, State flags, and organization or institutional flags are to be dipped as a mark of honor.

(a) The flag should never be displayed with the union down save as a signal of dire distress.

(b) The flag should never touch anything beneath it, such as the ground, the floor, water, or merchandise.

(c) The flag should never be carried flat or horizontally, but always aloft and free.

(d) The flag should never be used as drapery of any sort whatsoever, never festooned, drawn back, nor up, in folds, but always allowed to fall free. Bunting of blue, white and red, always arranged with the blue above, the white in the middle, and the red below, should be used for covering a speaker's desk, draping the front of a platform, and for decoration in general.

(e) The flag should never be fastened, displayed, used, or stored in such a manner as will permit it to be easily torn, soiled, or damaged in any way.

(f) The flag should never be used as a covering for a ceiling.

(g) The flag should never be used as a receptacle for receiving, holding, carrying, or delivering anything.

(h) The flag should never have placed upon it, nor on any part of it, nor attached to it any mark, insignia, letter, word, figure, design, picture, or drawing of any nature.

(i) The flag should never be used for advertising purposes in any manner whatsoever. It should not be embroidered on such articles as cushions or handkerchiefs and the like, printed or otherwise impressed on paper napkins or boxes or anything that is designed for temporary use and discard; or used as any portion of a costume or athletic uniform. Advertising signs should not be fastened to a staff or halyard from which the flag is flown.

(j) The flag, when it is in such condition that it is no longer a fitting emblem for display, should be destroyed in a dignified way, preferably by burning.

Sec. 5. That during the ceremony of hoisting or lowering the flag or when the flag is passing in a parade or in a review, all persons present should face the flag, stand at attention, and salute. Those present in uniform should render the military salute. When not in uniform, men should remove the headdress with the right hand holding it at the left shoulder, the hand being over the heart. Men without hats should salute in the same manner. Aliens should stand at attention. Women should salute by placing the right hand over the heart. The salute to the flag in the moving column should be rendered at the moment the flag passes.

Sec. 6. That when the national anthem is played and the flag is not displayed all present should stand and face toward the music. Those in uniform should salute at the first note of the anthem, retaining this position until the last note. All others should stand at attention, men removing the headdress. When the flag is displayed, all present should face the flag and salute.

Sec. 7. That the pledge of allegiance to the flag, "I pledge allegiance to the flag of the United States of America and to the Republic for which it stands, one Nation (under God) indivisible, with liberty and justice for all," be rendered by standing with the right hand over the heart. However, civilians will always show full respect to the flag when the pledge is given by merely standing at attention, men removing the headdress. Persons in uniform shall render the military salute.

Sec. 8. Any rule or custom pertaining to the display of the flag of the United States of America, set forth herein, may be altered, modified, or repealed, or additional rules with respect thereto may be prescribed, by the Commander in Chief of the Army and Navy of the United States, whenever he deems it appropriate or desirable; and any such alteration or additional rule shall be set forth in a proclamation.

NOTES ON FLAG LAWS

It might be noted that it is not improper to use a flag with the incorrect number of stars on it until it wears out, and that soiled or worn flags may be washed or dry cleaned to keep them neat until they are worn-out, at which point they should be destroyed.

GENERAL FLAG CEREMONY

NECESSARY MATERIALS: One American Flag; five red flag sashes (long enough to be tied around waists of participants)

The following flag raising and lowering ceremony is used in scout camps and can work for any interested group. Have nonparticipants assemble around flagpole in a horseshoe formation. Flag bearer and attendants line up in formation. Caller says, "Horseshoe attention." All in horseshoe come to attention with arms at their sides and eyes on the flag company. Caller says, "Color Guard, attention!" Color Guard moves from "at-ease" position of feet apart and arms clasped behind them to position with feet together and arms at sides. (Meanwhile flag bearer has arms in front holding the flag which is folded in a triangle, point facing the flagpole.) Caller says, "Color Guard, advance!" Color guard begins its walk toward the flagpole, beginning with the right foot, in unison. Color guard walks toward pole, then stops about five feet short of flagpole. At this point, when lowering the flag, the color guard would salute the flag (hand over heart salute), as the flag would already be on the pole. After color guard has stopped in front of the pole in the morning, the caller says, "Color Guard, post the colors!" In the evening, the caller says, "Color Guard, retire the colors!" In the morning, the flag bearer would then walk toward the pole with the assistant to his or her right, hand over the flag, unhook the ropes, and while the color bearer prepares the flag clips, the assistant unfolds the flag. (Note that the flag should ALWAYS go up unfurled.) The flag should be raised quickly in the morning, and lowered slowly in the evening. In the morning, the observers salute the flag from the time the first clip is put on the flag, until the flag reaches the top of the pole; in the evening, they salute from the time the flag first starts down the pole until the last clip is unhooked. In the morning, the color guard falls back into position after the flag rope has been tied, and salutes. If the pledge of allegiance is given, it should be given in the morning after the color guard have given their salute; in the evening, it should be given after the color guard have given their salute, before the call to retire the colors is issued. In the evening, after the flag is down and unhooked, the color guard may either fold the flag or carry it out to their starting position unfurled to be folded later. After all this has been done, the color guard is back to its place five feet from the pole. The caller says: "Color Guard, dismissed," in the morning only. In the evening, the call is, "Color Guard, retreat." After the color guard gets back to their original position, the caller says, "Horseshoe dismissed," and the horseshoe members file out.

There should always be absolute silence during a flag ceremony except for the caller, or unless the pledge is said or a song is sung. Eyes should be on the flag at all times, and posture should reflect respect. The sashes which are worn by the flag company are always tied on the left around the waist, except for the flag bearer who wears his or her sash across the right shoulder and tied at the left waist. Here is a review of the caller's commands:

Morning Flag	**Evening Flag**
Horseshoe Attention	Horseshoe attention
Color Guard Attention	Color Guard Attention
Color Guard Advance	Color Guard Advance
Color Guard Post the Colors	Color Guard Salute
Color Guard Salute	Pledge of Allegiance
Pledge of Allegiance	Color Guard Retire the Colors
Color Guard Dismissed	Fold the flag
Horseshoe Dismissed	Color Guard retreat
	Horseshoe Dismissed

HOW TO FOLD A FLAG:

It is much easier to show than to tell how this is

done. A very good description of the process is found in *Camp Counseling*, by A. Viola Mitchell, Ida B. Crawford, and Julia D. Robberson:

> "... the Color Guard fold it lengthwise, first into halves, then into fourths. The two Guards at the end away from the stars then begin to fold it into triangles, starting with a triangular fold across the end and continuing with triangular folds back and forth until it is completely folded into one triangle with stars on both sides. They then hand it to the Color Bearer to carry."

When the flag has been folded, it should look neat and there should be no red showing.

Crafts

During colonial days being able to make candles, quilts or a basket were necessary skills. Even then, a decorative touch was added to make the article attractive. Today opportunities are almost unlimited to work with crafts. Why not turn your hand to soap-making, stenciling, pomanders or decorating for a colonial Christmas?

122

14 Crafts: Candle-making, Basketry, Embroidery, Samplers, Quilting, Soap-making, Stenciling

CRAFTS WERE ESSENTIAL IN COLONIAL TIMES, more for the useful products they produced than for the enjoyment they provided, although then as now a well-wrought item brought a sense of satisfaction and accomplishment.

As the Bicentennial approaches, there is increasing interest in simple folk arts, in doing things with one's own hands. You'll find some intriguing suggestions here for getting back to basics.

HAND-DIPPED CANDLES

Candles were used extensively in colonial America for lighting. A great many pieces of colonial literature and countless documents were written by the light of candles. The Declaration of Independence was signed by candlelight and the first reception at the White House in 1809 was lighted by a thousand candles.

Candles were normally made at home, not bought. Early candles were made by dipping a string, or wick, repeatedly in melted tallow—a kind of refined animal fat. The candles were dipped 20-30 times until they reached the desired size. Some early candles gave off heavy soot and noxious fumes, depending on the type of animal fat used for tallow. When properly made, hand-dipped candles give off a brighter, clearer, more even light than molded candles. They are the aristocrats of the candle world.

AGE GROUP: 8 or older

MATERIALS: Electric burner or flame for heating wax; work tables; narrow, deep tin can; coffee cans in which water is boiled; beeswax (preferable) or paraffin, or half of each; candle wicks; natural coloring agents (optional); small weights (nails are good); newspapers for protecting floor; sand or baking soda for fire emergencies

DIRECTIONS: Spread newspapers over work area. Break up wax into 1-inch pieces and place in one of cans; add coloring if desired. Melt wax in double boiler. Fill second can with cold water. Cut wicking 4-6 inches longer than the length of candle you desire; tie nail on one end for weight. When wax is melted stir to insure even coloring if using color. Hold end of wick without nail in your fingers and dip the nail and wick into melted wax but do not let nail hit bottom of can. Remove wick and nail from can and allow wax on wick to harden for few minutes, then repeat dipping. After 3-4 dips, or when wick is fairly stiff, cut nail off wick with scissors. Don't try to untie nail from wick as you might break layers of wax off. Continue to dip, without letting end of candle hit bottom of can. After each dip let wax harden in air for a count of 20 and dip candle in cold water for a count of 10. Dry off candle very gently with rag and repeat entire process. Dipping in water may be omitted, but then candle must harden in air for 20-30 minutes before re-dipping in melted wax. Dipping continues until candle is size desired; then dip once more in melted wax but not in water. Most candles require 30-40 dips for good size. Hang candle by wick on clothesline (with clothespin) to thoroughly harden; this usually takes about 12 hours at room temperature (70 degrees). Clean up.

SAFETY: Never melt wax over *open* flame; it is highly flammable. Hot wax can cause bad burns. Use baking soda or sand to douse fires. Never let unsupervised or very young children make candles. Lit candles present a fire hazard unless properly used.

SCENTING: Scents can be added to melted wax just prior to dipping. Use oil-based scents; commercial ones are available. Also, any oil-based perfume may be used. Aromatic leaves such as eucalyptus, citrus, pine, and citronella are other possibilities; leaves should be shredded and tied loosely in bag of cheesecloth. Push bag below surface of melted wax and let remain for 10 minutes. Then begin dipping.

SUPPLIES: Candlemaking supplies may be purchased at most hobby and craft shops. If you have difficulty locating supplies contact one of these dealers:

American Handicrafts Co.
1001 Foch Street
Fort Worth, Texas 76017

Wicks and Wax Candle Shop
350 North Atlantic Avenue
Cocoa Beach, Florida 32931

Pourette Manufacturing Co.
6818 Roosevelt Way
Seattle, Washington

The Candle Mill
East Arlington, Vermont
05252

General Supplies Co.
P. O. Box 338
Fallbrook, California

Candlelite House
4228 East Easter Place
Littleton, Colorado 80102

PETALED CANDLES*

MATERIALS: Newspaper; waxed paper; double boiler or large can and larger can; stick for stirring; candy thermometer; corn oil; electric soldering iron or large nail; salt or baking soda; four spoons in graduated sizes—doll-size (or demitasse), teaspoon, tablespoon, and large serving spoon; 1 pound paraffin wax; tapers—two 15 inches long, one 10 inches long.

Candles are decorated with rows of petals formed in bowl of spoon; the size of petal is determined by the size of spoon used. To make petal, heat wax to approximately 180°F. Grease bowl of spoon lightly with corn oil. Using another spoon, pour a small amount of wax into oiled spoon bowl; rotate spoon to coat bowl evenly. Remove wax from spoon while wax is still warm by sliding it off with your thumb. Pinch petal at one end to complete shape of white petals; curl petals to form rose petal shapes.

To attach petals, use soldering iron or heated nail tip to melt vertical grooves for each row around taper and to soften the ends of petals. Insert one petal end into each groove. If petal does not adhere well, apply a small amount of wax at the joint. Let wax harden and attach next petal around.

*Reproduced with permission from the 1974, Fall/Winter issue of *McCall's Needlework and Crafts Magazine*.

Follow directions below.

TREE CANDLES: Each row is made up of eight petals. The 15" tapers each have 10 rows of petals starting 4" down from the top. The 10" taper has eight rows of petals starting 1-1/2" down from the top. Use the smallest spoon for the first three rows of petals, use the next size spoon for rows 4 and 5, the next size for rows 6 and 7, the largest spoon for row 8 of the 10" taper and rows 8, 9, and 10 for the 15" tapers. When adhering the second row of petals, space them alternately between the petals of the first row. Continue in same manner for remaining rows (see illustration).

ICE LIGHTS (TIN LANTERNS)

MATERIALS: Paper for pattern; pencil; masking tape; an absorbent cloth; hammer; nails of different sizes; assortment of cans

DIRECTIONS: Fill each can with water to 1/8-inch below rim and place in freezer for about 2 days. For each can cut paper to fit can's sides, then draw design. Wrap the pattern tightly around the can and secure with two or three lengths of masking tape wrapped around the length of the can. Place can on side over folded, absorbent cloth. With hammer and nail punch along the lines of the pattern. For each hole, tap the nail firmly two or three times, making sure it reaches through the can to the ice. To vary the size of the holes, use different sized nails or punching tools. Large holes permit more light to come through while smaller holes make more intricate patterns. After removing ice, secure a candle in the lantern with floral or modeling clay. If bottom of can swells during freezing, hammer back down when finished. Use seamless aluminum funnels for tops.

PAUL REVERE'S LANTERN ("TINWARE")

AGE GROUP: 8 or older

MATERIALS: Heavy-duty aluminum foil; nail; screwdrivers (regular and Phillips); pen; metal

nail file; other objects that can punch different shaped holes; scissors; felt-tip pen; scrap paper; masking tape; box top from shoe box; small votive-type candle

DIRECTIONS: Copy patterns from figures 1 and 3 onto scrap paper—this will be your pattern for aluminum foil cutting. Using paper pattern, trace and draw design with felt-tip pen, then cut out the top and bottom of the lantern from a piece of foil. Tape the foil pieces to the edges of the shoe box so it is taut (see figure 2). Following your design, use various tools to punch through the foil. The different objects make different shapes. After all holes are punched, carefully remove tape and pull foil free of the box. Cut slits into the foil near edge.

Figure 1.

tab

fold line

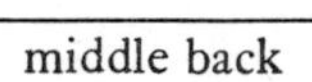

middle back

fold line

slit

Push the top tab through the slit and fold it back. Repeat the process for the remaining pattern piece. When top and bottom are completed, place them on a flat surface with the glass-encased candle inside (see figure 4). *Note:* When candle is lit, adequate supervision of children in area is essential for safety.

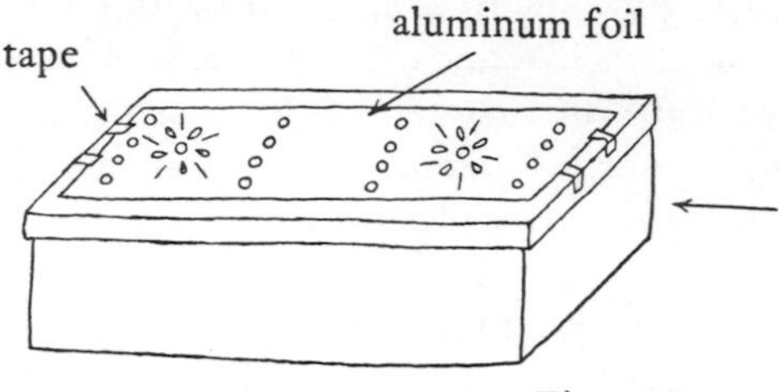

Figure 2.

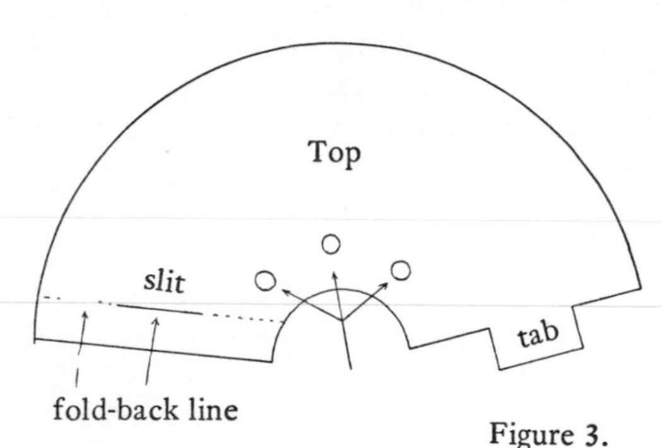

Figure 3.

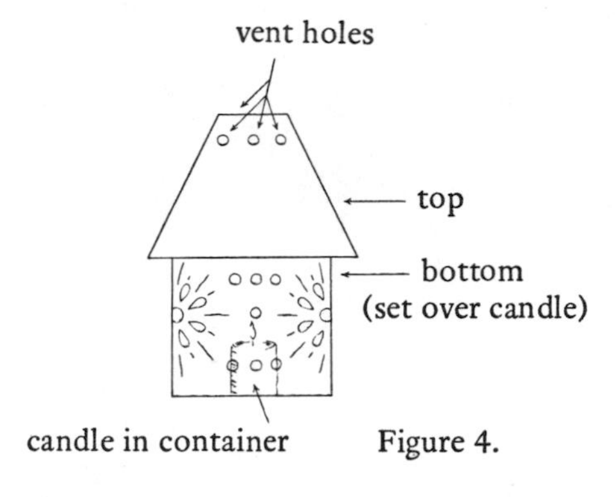

Figure 4.

SILHOUETTES

This is an old craft that was popular in America in the 1700's.

AGE GROUP: 6 or older

MATERIALS: Bright light (100 watt or brighter electric bulb); white and black paper; tape; pencil; scissors; chair

DIRECTIONS: Place the white paper on the wall and secure with tape. Seat subject in front of paper. Place the light opposite the subject and wall. Adjust light so that sharp shadow is thrown by subject's head. Using pencil, carefully trace outline of the shadow. Let subject cut out his own profile, which can then be placed on black paper for contrast; or, place white silhouette on black paper and retrace, then cut out of black paper. Gold and silver inks were used in the 1700's and 1800's.

TRADITIONAL HAND HOOKING

AGE GROUP: 8-12

MATERIALS: Yarn or thin strips of wool; crochet hook—one per child; embroidery hoop—one per child; burlap—one piece per child; scissors

DIRECTIONS: Cut piece of burlap so that it fits in the embroidery hoop. Pull it taut. Cut a piece of wool about 12 inches long. Basic stitch:

(1) Hold wool or yarn under the burlap in the embroidery hoop. From the top of the burlap insert the crochet hook.
(2) Lay wool into the hook and pull through top of burlap. Let form a small loop about 1/4-inch high.
(3) Insert needle in next hole and pull up another loop of yarn, as with first.
(4) Go into each hole if possible, or almost every hole if wool is thick—not too many, as material will pucker, however. Pictures, rugs, pot holders, pillows, or large group projects can be made.

BASKETRY

Basketry is one of the most ancient and universal crafts. American Indians were excellent basket weavers. Colonists from almost every country brought basketry skills with them. In 1776 in this country baskets were used to store and protect goods being transported as well as for domestic purposes.

MATERIALS: Several different materials are used for basketmaking, including willow or osier, cane and wicker, seagrass, reed, raffia, and rushes. It is possible to obtain most of these materials in various thicknesses, lengths and textures, and also in almost any color, as they are often specially dyed. Basketwork usually looks most effective in the natural color, from cream to soft brown, rather than when bright colors are used.

Reed is probably the best known basket weaving material. It is made from rattan, a vine that abounds in the tropical forests and swamps of the Malay Peninsula and it sometimes attains a length of several hundred feet. The hard glossy outside covering of the rattan is removed, split into narrow strips and used in weaving chair seats. The core or pithy center is divided by machinery into numerous spaghetti-like strands of 12 to 15 feet in length, which are then known as reed. This is graded according to thickness from No. 00 to No. 17, the lowest number being the smallest and the most expensive. The material is bunched into hanks of 1 pound weight and is sold by the pound.

Reed has to be soaked before using to make it pliable and to keep it from breaking. Sizes 4 and 5 should be soaked in hot or tepid water 15 or 20 minutes; sizes 1, 2, and 3 have to be soaked for only about 10 minutes and size 00 merely has to be dipped in water.

Raffia, a product of Madagascar, is made from the outer cuticle of a palm peculiar to that island. It is soft and pliable and easily manipulated by children.

Wicker is a rather general term applied mainly to willow. However, the expression wickerware includes many kinds of basketry.

TOOLS: The tools required for the art of basketry are simple and inexpensive. For various types of basket weaving the tools needed are: a hand drill with various size bits, a table-mounted vise grip, snips, a ruler, screwdriver, coping saw, pencil, compass, pocket knife, hammer, punch, and alcohol lamp. The alcohol lamp can be made from an old oil can, the spout being cut off short and a wick inserted. A small hole must be punctured into the spout to admit the necessary air. If all of these tools are assembled the work will be expedited from the start.

In almost every vicinity there are natural materials that may be used instead of the commercial ones. This may enable you to devise an entirely different basket from any you have seen. The use of homegrown materials offers a very wide field for experiment.

The Indians make use of yucca. Both the long and short pine needles may be used. Rushes and many tough grasses that grow on marshy lands are useful in basketry.

CHILD'S INTERMEDIATE BASKET

The materials required are: one piece of 3/8-inch plywood, 8x8 inches for bottom of basket; 28 pieces of No. 4 round reed, 10 inches long, for spokes; No. 3 round reed for weavers; and No. 2 round reed for braid around bottom edge.

First prepare wood for base by cutting a circle 8-inches in diameter. Next, draw a circle 1/4 inch from edge of board. Drill 28 holes 7/8 inches apart to hold spokes of basket. Use a 7/64 inch bit. After all holes are drilled, shellac the entire board to protect from dampness. Apply a drop of glue to the tips of the 10 inch pieces of No. 4 reed and insert one spoke in each hole, so they all bend outward. Soak the No. 3 reed in hot water for a few minutes. This makes it flexible and easy to handle; if it is soaked too long, it will become brittle again.

Work in any weave desired to a height of 4 or 5 inches and finish with an open border.

WEAVES

Here is a description of the weaves generally used. By modifying and combining them, a large number of designs may be made.

SINGLE WEAVE: This simple weave is not used much, as it is slow. Using one weaver and starting behind any of the spokes, you go in front of the next spoke and behind the third, continuing in this manner until finished. The single weave requires an odd number of spokes.

DOUBLE SINGLE WEAVE: This is done the same way as the single weave, except two weavers are used side by side.

TRIPLE SINGLE WEAVE: The same as the first two, except three weavers are used, giving the effect of a ribbon. These weaves are occasionally used to break the monotony of another weave.

PAIRING WEAVE: This is one of the most popular styles of weaving. It is simple and fast. Two weavers are used to bind each warp spoke, with weavers twisting between the spokes. Each strand continues in and out. Where one goes in front of a spoke, the other goes behind and so on.

DOUBLE PAIRING WEAVE: Very similar to the pairing weave except double strands are held flat and woven in and out together.

TRIPLE WEAVE: This is strongest of the common weaves and very popular in basket work. Place three weavers behind three spokes. Hold them in place with the left hand. Place the left weavers in front of the two spokes to the right, back of the third and then out to the front. Repeat this operation, always working with the left strand.

STARTING A STRAND: When starting a strand, the weaver is always placed behind the spoke overlapping it about 1/4-inch so it will not pull out.

ENDING A STRAND: When ending a strand the weaver is always ended behind the spoke, giving it about 1/4-inch overlap. The weave should always be ended directly above its starting point.

MAKING A SPLICE: When you come to the end of one strand you have to add a new one. The finished strand is cut off behind a spoke and the beginning of a new strand laid on top of the other and behind the same spoke, the two strand ends crossing each other in back of the same spoke. Hold the new end down with the left hand until you have this strand through a few spokes to fasten it in place. The important thing is to make the splice behind the spoke and not in front of it.

OPEN BORDER: This border may be made in single, double or triple style.

SINGLE OPEN BORDER: A spoke, after being thoroughly soaked, is bent over sharply and its end inserted through the weave alongside of the next spoke. This spoke is likewise bent down and inserted next to the following spoke and so on. The single type of border is rather weak and for this reason the double and triple borders are much preferred.

DOUBLE OPEN BORDER: The spoke that is bent over is inserted in the weave alongside the second spoke. The next spoke is similarly inserted two spokes away so the loops overlap. The bent spoke is always brought in front of the next one, so they will all overlap uniformly.

TRIPLE OPEN BORDER: Each spoke is inserted alongside the third successive spoke—skipping two spokes. This border is well interwoven, good-looking, and strong. To facilitate inserting the spokes through the weave, their ends may be pointed with a penknife. It may also be necessary at times to spread the weave apart with an awl or an ordinary ice pick.

FINISH THE BASKET by tacking a piece of decorative braid around the base.

SAMPLERS

HISTORY: The word sampler comes from the Latin derivative "exemplar," defined by Palsgrave as "an example for a woman to work by." The sampler originated in early America and served as a substitute for the rare and costly pattern books which only the wealthy could afford. Thus, the sampler became a record of the various patterns and stitches of the period. In some cases, it was used to record family dates: births, deaths, marriages and names of family members.

The sampler was generally worked by young girls. They used a piece of square linen or silk cloth to demonstrate their embroidery skills and to create new and different stitches. The small fingers patiently worked, under the watchful eyes of their elders, to improve their stitchery. The many sampler patterns were usually handed down from generation to generation and from mother to daughter and teacher to student. Each sampler was signed and dated by the needleworker.

The patterns chosen for the sampler included various letter forms in cross stitch, strawberries and other fruits, roses, geometric designs, figures, the schoolhouse she attended, and numerous seasonal scenes. For the figures of people, real hair was used and sometimes the faces were hand painted for a more delicate effect. Sequins were also used for more decoration. The 17th century samplers were long and narrow with the upper section in a band design of fruit and flowers or geometric designs. The lower half consisted of a scene or a pious verse.

Later samplers became longer and broader and developed a border design. In the mid-18th century, a distinctive type of sampler evolved. The edges were of floral borders with the center divided into squares, in which floral motifs and verses were embroidered in alternating squares. At this time an emphasis on special and religious verses developed and became extremely popular. These mottoes and prayers were intended to instill good morals in youthful minds.

MATERIALS: When the colonists first arrived in the new world, their belongings were quite limited. The materials used for embroidery were usually homemade and treasured. It was not unusual for a mother to hand down her sewing needle to her daughter for her first sampler. Indians used a pierced fish bone to sew with and dyed porcupine quills for thread. A woman would treasure her needle, for it was generally imported from Europe and expensive. The cloth used for the sampler was also homemade; women would weave wool from their sheep and grow flax for linen. It took 1-1/2 years from planting flax to spinning it into linen thread and weaving it into cloth.

DYES: Most households were equipped with indigo tubs in the kitchen and a dye pot hung over a fire in the backyard. Like many other skills, this dying technique was learned from Indian women. When black walnut husks were boiled they made brown dye, pokeberries were used for purple, spring butternut shells dyed light green, onion skins or goldenrod made yellow and indigo was blue. One would acquire tones from light to dark by simmering the skeins for a longer or shorter period of time, or redye for different colors. After dying, alum or salt was used to set the color. Even though primitive methods were used, this era was the most productive time for hand stitchery.

FABRIC: The thread and fabric should be suitable to each other and the style of design. A moderate open weave is best. Technically this is described by the space produced by the angle of the vertical warp (═══) and the horizontal weft (||||||||||) so that threads in the

Satin Stitch: Work straight stitches across the shape as shown. If desired, chain stitch or running stitch may be worked first to form a padding underneath, for a raised effect. Care must be taken to keep a good edge. Do not make the stitches too long, as they could be pulled out of position. Satin stitch can also be worked over counted threads of even weave fabric. In this case, the stitches are taken over the desired number of threads and are worked one stitch between each two adjacent threads of the fabric.

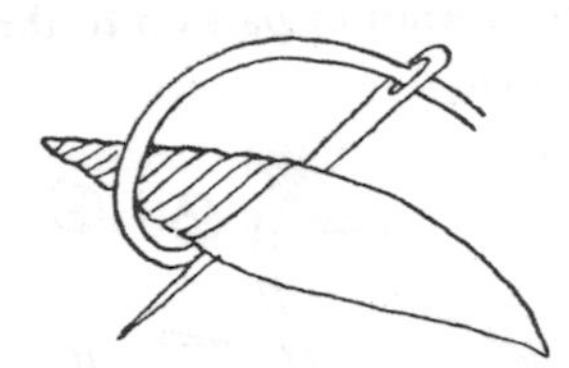

Scroll Stitch: This stitch is worked from left to right. The working thread is looped to the right, then back to the left on the fabric. Inside this loop the needle takes a small slanting stitch to the left under the line of the design with the thread of the loop under the needle point. The thread is then pulled through. The stitches should be used as a border.

Stem Stitch: Work from left to right, taking regular, slightly slanting stitches along the line of the design. The thread always emerges on the left side of the previous stitch. This stitch is used for flower stems, outlines, etc. It can also be used as a filling, rows of close stem stitch being worked around a shape until it is filled in completely.

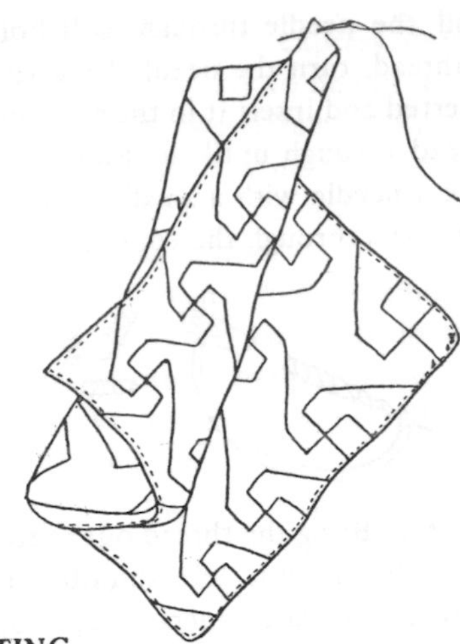

QUILTING

Quilting originally meant using a small running or back stitch to join two layers of material together. A layer of batting or padding is usually between the cover (top layer) and the backing (bottom layer). However, it is not required. The stitches create a raised pattern on the cover and the backing of the piece, and secure the two or three layers of material so that shifting does not occur.

Tufting is an offshoot of quilting; it is a technique using yarn or thread to tie the three layers of material (cover, batting, and bottom) together.

Trapunto is another variation of the quilting technique. It utilizes a very loosely woven backing which is quilted to a tightly woven cover (there is no interlining). The quilting is usually done in delicate floral patterns. Then selected parts of the pattern such as flower petals, leaves, or scrolls are stuffed from the back (through the loosely woven backing) with little bits of batting or thin cording. Thus a raised pattern is achieved in only specific places.

Embroidery, applique, piecing, and patchwork are other techniques which have been incorporated into the art of quiltmaking, so the meaning of quilting has expanded to signify the use of any technique to make a cover and attach it to a backing (even if they are attached only on the outer edges). In the purest sense of the word, however, quilting still means only the use of a running or back stitch to join a cover, batting, and a backing.

THE HISTORY OF QUILTING IN AMERICA:

The American pioneer situation spawned the unique American art of quilting and patchwork in the United States. Living in relative isolation on the new continent where fabric was not abundant encouraged the pioneers to save and treasure every scrap of material. Worn clothes were carefully patched to lengthen their life. When they finally were discarded, the good material was salvaged to piece and patch other garments. Out of necessity, pioneer women started piecing small scraps of fabric together to form the covers of quilts. Quilts were a vital means of keeping a home and its inhabitants warm (especially in New England). Patchwork combines thrift and creativity, two attributes highly valued in America, to make a useful and attractive article. Patchwork was often the only form of recreation and self-expression for a pioneer woman.

In the late 1600's, however, fabric was more abundant in America and some women had cloth to spare. Exotic but expensive fabrics were available from the East Indies and Europe. Richly hand-blocked and painted fabrics (palampores) from India, featuring intricate figures and shapes, were very much in vogue during this period. Because it was so expensive, small pieces were bought or scraps were used. The figures and shapes on the fabric were cut out and appliqued to larger, less expensive pieces of material.

From this point on Americans used their ingenuity to combine available materials using sewing techniques. The entire family, even husbands, took part in designing and making quilts. Quilting spanned the history of America's development, moving and growing with the people.

QUILTING FOR GROUPS:

Quilting is one of the more beautiful crafts, and there are a number of ways to apply quilting to useful or playful things. Possibilities include stuffed toys (especially near Christmas), clothing, potholders, pillows, wall hangings, headscarves, purses, pictures, etc. And there is an unlimited number of traditional patterns besides the ones you can design.

This can appeal to people of all age groups who can sew a button on a shirt without too much loss of blood. It seems an ideal way to get senior citizens and younger people together—teaching and learning from one another. A revival of the old-time sewing (quilting) bees could be a social event too.

QUILTING MATERIALS AND EQUIPMENT:

Fabrics: Fabrics need not be expensive or new but must be in good condition. You will need fabric for the three parts of a quilt—top, backing, and filling. For the top, most experts advise using the same kinds of fabrics together on any one design. For instance, linens and cottons go together, silks and satins, etc. The most common quilts use gingham, light chintz, percale, calico, broadcloth, and shirting. If you choose a fabric that can be laundered, be sure that it is preshrunk and all the colors are fast. A general rule to follow is to use the very best materials that you can afford for any handwork. Firm weave in whatever grade of fabric you choose is important, especially when cutting geometric designs.

For the backing, muslin, broadcloth, or percale are recommended. You can find especially made cotton or fluffier dacron filling or batting in fabric departments. An old blanket can also be used as the filling. The warmth of the quilt will depend on the thickness and kind of interlining you use.

Measure all materials carefully to be sure you have too much rather than too little. Colors are difficult to match.

Needles: Use fine, short needles, No. 9 or 8.

Thread: Usually No. 50 white for piecing, finer or matching mercerized tints for applique. For machine piecing use finer thread, perhaps 70. Numbers 50 or 60 are the standard quilting threads, white in almost all cases, although quilting on fine satin is lovely in No. 70. A No. 50 crochet twist in colors is effective for quilting on silk or rayons. Read the label to be sure that your thread is waxed or is resistant to knotting.

Frame: The authentic way to quilt is to have a large frame into which the whole coverlet is stretched. It is constructed from four planed pine strips 2 inches wide by 3/4 inch or 1 inch thick. These strips are cut into two lengths: usually 9 feet and 4-6 feet. Clamps hold the corners secure. After the layers are attached to the frame, the basting and actual quilting takes place.

Hoop: A substitute for the frame. It is easily handled and can be moved around, but it takes greater care when basting and quilting.

QUILTED POTHOLDER

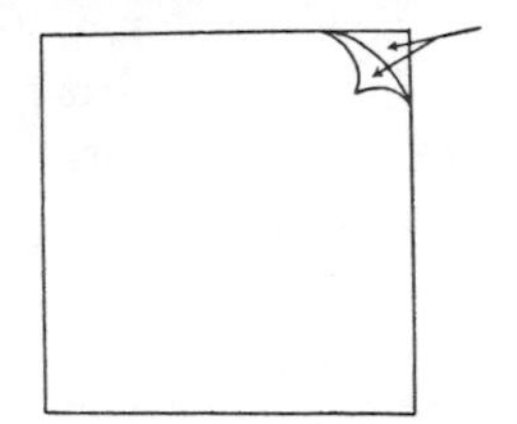

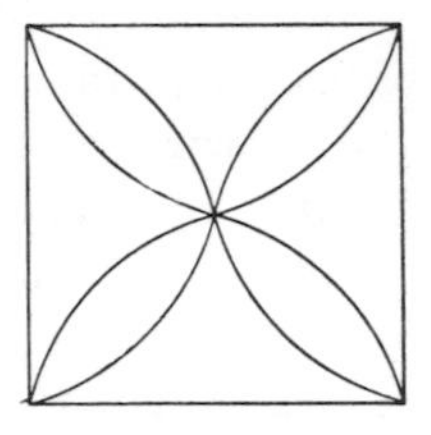

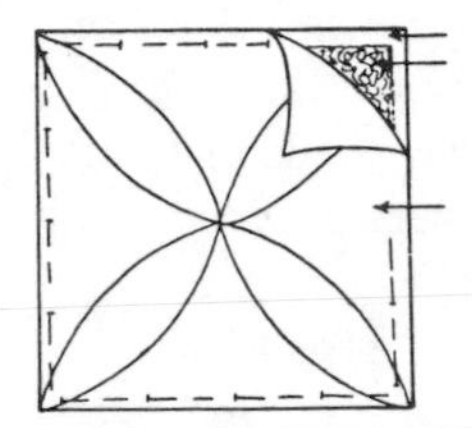

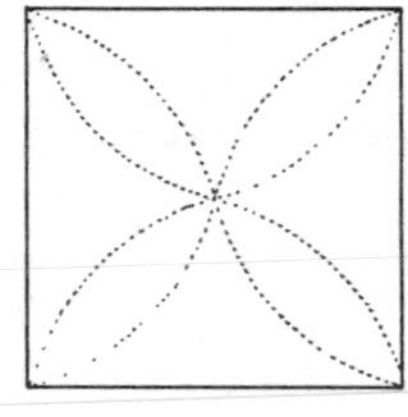

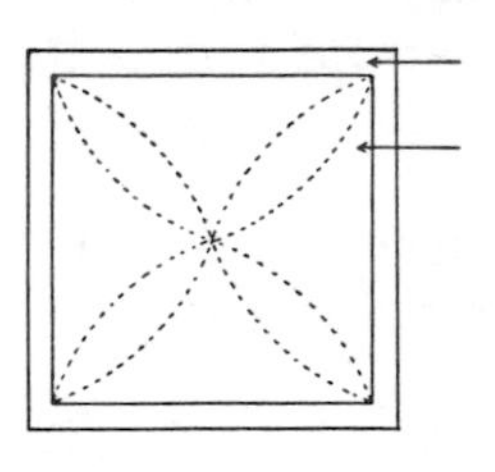

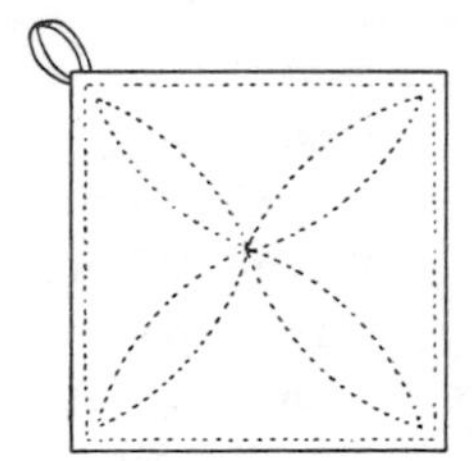

AGE GROUP: 8-12

MATERIALS: Two pieces cotton fabric about 8 inches square; cotton or polyester batting (or cotton pieces or balls); sewing needle; pins; scissors; dressmaker's carbon paper; quilting thread

DIRECTIONS: Cut two squares of fabric 8 by 8 inches. Sketch design on paper and transfer to fabric, using carbon paper. Face wrong side of unmarked fabric up on the table. Lay strips of batting on the fabric; cut approximately 1/4-inch shorter. Place marked fabric with right side up on top of batting. Pin these 3 layers together (1 pin per inch). Following the outlined pattern, make tiny running stitches that go through the 3 thicknesses. Remember to knot your thread every time you use a new piece and to check both sides of the potholder to see if the stitches are visible on both sides. Try to keep stitches equal in length. When pattern is completely stitched, turn under the raw open edges by tucking edge under so no edge shows. Take the bottom remaining cotton and tuck it in next to the other piece of fabric. Do a running stitch around the edge of the potholder and pierce through all the layers so stitches are visible on both sides. Attach loop to hang.

HOMEMADE SOAP

In colonial days, all grease was saved—it was a valuable and useful commodity, and the basis for soap. Wood ashes were the source of soap's other principal ingredient, lye. The grease and lye were boiled together in a big iron kettle out in the open; the odor was highly unpleasant. The mixture was constantly stirred and cooked into a harsh, soft soap. For some reason, this process wasn't always successful, so neighbors wished each other luck with their soapmaking.

COLD WATER SOAP

AGE GROUP: At least 9, with *careful* supervision.

MATERIALS: 13 ounces flake lye; 2-1/2 pints cold water; 6 pounds purified lard; oil-based scents (optional); large cooking utensil—not aluminum; stirrer

DIRECTIONS: Be sure work area is well-ventilated; the fumes are irritating. Measure 2-1/2 pints cold water into kettle or other utensil. Slowly add one can of lye and stir until dissolved. Allow mixture to cool. To purify lard, measure waste grease and boil it in double its volume of water. Skim off 6 pounds clean grease. Allow to cool to lukewarm. Pour lard into the lye mixture, stirring to insure even mixing. Add scents now if desired. Stir thoroughly for 15 minutes (it will look like turkey gravy). When *thick*, scoop into cardboard or cloth-lined tin pans. Allow to harden, cut when hard. Makes a useful brown soap good for all kinds of washing.

GRAVESTONE RUBBINGS
AGE GROUP: 7 or older
MATERIALS: Silk span; India ink; rag (wad from old T-shirt); wax crayons (dark); large pad or roll of string, lightweight paper (newsprint, rice paper, etc.); roll of masking tape.
DIRECTIONS: Silk span may be purchased at hobby stores.

Select the surface you wish to copy. Try to find a stone that is well preserved rather than one that has been worn down or has flaws or a rough surface. Be sure that it is free from foreign matter; if any is present, brush it away carefully without damaging the stone. Crop any grass that might get in the way.

Tape the paper with masking tape to the top of the stone. Then tape it to one side. With your hand smooth it across the surface of the stone. Hold it in place as you tape the other side. Keep smoothing it, removing and replacing the tape until the paper is taut over the whole surface of the stone.

Remove the wrapper from part of the crayon and use a broad edge of it. Rub lightly from the center out until the design is established on your paper. Stroke constantly in the same direction. Once the design is lightly drawn the way you wish it to appear, go over it again, working in from the edges.

If using silk span, attach it in same manner as paper. When *smoothly* placed, dab a small piece of T-shirt that has been dampened with India ink over the silk span surface.

You may wish to accent the design by pressing more heavily in certain sections rather than others. Before finishing, step back and check over the rubbing as a whole to see if you have attained the evenness of color you desire. Carefully peel the masking tape from the rubbing and then remove both from the stone.

Before making a final rubbing to exhibit you will want to make a proof to try out the surface from which you will work. Use less expensive paper (newsprint is fine for this proof). Make a quick rubbing (you will not need to be as careful as you will be in making the final rubbing) and study it for areas you wish to avoid in the final print.

You may discover large negative areas, cracks or depressions you do not wish to print. Remember the carving is fairly shallow and care must be taken to avoid printing large background areas.

You can make corrections after the print is removed from the rubbing surface but this is difficult to do because it is almost impossible to erase crayon. A razor blade can be used to scrape off crayon and white paint can be used to try to cover up the spot.

It is much easier to add color. Do this by holding the paper over another surface as close to the original as possible. You may wish to make a stronger contrast in an area where the contrast is weak due to the rough texture of the original surface. Fasten the paper to a slightly smoother surface and touch up the area carefully.

Two rubbings from colonial tombstones read:

Herein lies Jonathan Rush
And this forever was his curse:
He always drew a royal flush
When he held an empty purse

Friends prepare
Yourself to follow me
As I now am, you
Soon will be

STENCILING
American stencilcraft was probably derived from European practices. Stenciling was applied to walls, floors, and furniture. Inspiration for designs came from field flowers, fruits, patriotic symbols, crewelwork, embroidery, and decorated pottery.
MATERIALS: Stencil board of good grade paper, e.g., manila; plate glass (or marble, masonite, etc.) for cutting surface; stencil knives and blades; carborundum block for keeping blades sharp; straight edge or rule; coloring brushes; sponges; drafting tape; white blotter. Paper must be treated: soak a rag in boiled linseed oil and turpentine and wipe it over

paper on both sides until saturated; hang to dry for 2 hours.

METHOD: Be sure all cutting surfaces are clean. Trim all edges of board so there is no less than 1 inch and no more than 2 inches around transferred design. The plate is always square or

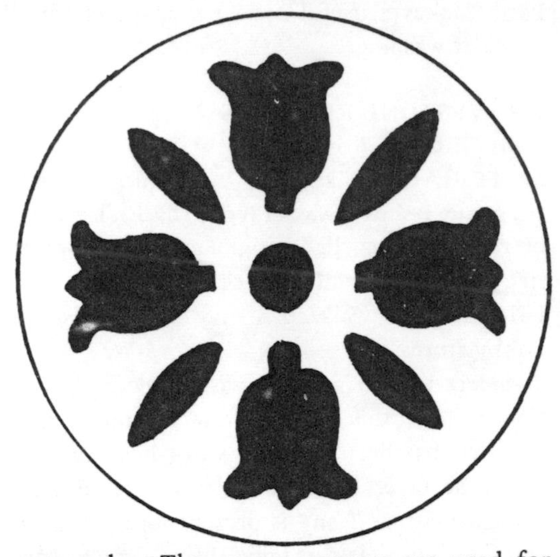

rectangular. The square corners are used for lining up the stencil plate with chalk guidelines. Place the stencil board on the cutting surface, but *do not* secure it. The stencil paper must be able to move freely, guided with the fingertips of your free hand. The paper should be capable of swinging around to accommodate the movement of the knife. Hold the knife as you would a pencil, only slightly more perpendicular. Grasp firmly but lightly and use the whole arm for action. Cut toward you, not away from you. Small details should be cut first. Cut all vertical lines, shift plate, and cut horizontal lines. When adjacent lines meet and form a corner or angle, cut slightly past the ends of the intersecting lines. This prevents ragged or whiskered corners. Coloring matter should be mixed to a fairly thick consistency; Japan paint, oil paint, acrylic, casein, stains, silk screen paint, textile ink or paint, or spray enamel may be used. Use drafting tape to secure plate to work surface. Brushes come in a variety of shapes and sizes; a stencil brush ideally receives coloring matter of flat bottom surface only—not sides. Use a white blotter underneath when stencilling fabric.

15 Give a Gift of Fragrance: Pomander, Potpourri and Sachet

POMANDER

"POMANDER"—THE WORD ITSELF stirs the imagination and conjures up visions of medieval pageantry, when the "pomme d'ambre," or apple of gold, was carried as a matter of course by the gallants and ladies at the court as a protection against infection or disease. The earliest pomanders were made of clay; one Spanish pomander was set with emeralds. The most popular pomander is the humble orange that has been "cloved." Its delicate and lasting aroma recalls the charm of an Old World garden.

OLD FASHIONED CHRISTMAS POMANDER BALLS

Start six weeks or so before Christmas, as the pomanders should age. These make wonderful gifts and stocking stuffers. Many homes have pomander balls hanging from beams in the ceiling to perfume the air with a lovely, old-fashioned fragrance.

MATERIALS: One pound long-stemmed cloves (for 10-12 balls); apples, oranges, crabapples, limes, lemons, or other fruit; 1/2-pound of mixed, ground spices (cinnamon predominating, also cloves, powdered ginger, freshly grated whole nutmeg; 2 ounces crushed orris root (from druggist)

DIRECTIONS: Work over a large surface of the fruit to prevent too much tension in one spot. Insert cloves closely with heads touching. Finish each ball within a day, before the skin starts to shrink and harden. Disregard small splits in skin; larger ones may be sewn together. Place spice mixture in large bowl; add fruits and turn until well-coated. Leave balls in mixture, stirring once each day until they begin to lose

the weight of the juice. To hang, thread a large-eyed needle with narrow velvet ribbon and run through the fruit about an inch from the top.

ROSE BEADS

AGE GROUP: 6 or older

MATERIALS: Large quantity of rose petals; 1 teaspoon salt for each quart of petals; food coloring (optional); food grinder; copper wire; cloth; few drops rose oil (optional); alcohol; olive oil

DIRECTIONS: Sprinkle rose petals with salt,

one teaspoon per quart of petals. If desired, color with liquid food coloring, but tint lightly. Run through fine blade of food grinder. To shape into beads, roll a small amount between the palms of the hands. Make the beads twice as large as you want them, since they will shrink to half the original size. Place on large platter so they do not touch, and dry partially in the sun for one day.

The following day, string beads on a copper wire about the thickness of a darning needle. Decorate by indenting with the fingers or making an impression on each end with a clove. Remove from wire, place in cloth sack, and polish by gently rubbing together. For scent, mix few drops of rose oil with alcohol, then sprinkle a small amount in the palms of the hands and rub the beads, turning them over until the oil is absorbed. Dry again, then soak in olive oil for several days. Wipe, dry, and string.

POTPOURRI (DRIED FLOWER PETALS)

AGE GROUP: 6 or older

MATERIALS: Flower petals (e.g., roses, geraniums, marigolds, honeysuckle, etc.); commercial or garden herbs such as mint, thyme, rosemary, sage, bay leaves, lavender; 1 pound table salt; large, lidded casserole; 2 ounces orris root (from druggist); 3 tablespoons brown sugar; 3-4 ounces crushed spices (e.g., whole cloves, nutmeg, cinnamon sticks); 1 ounce benzoin or 1 tablespoon brandy (optional).

DIRECTIONS: Strip off petals and spread to dry in shady place. Turn several times a day for a week to hasten drying. Put 2 quarts of petals and a mixture of herbs in a lidded casserole large enough to permit easy stirring. Pour 1 pound of table salt over the mixture and close the casserole. Mix several times a day for a week. Lift petals from casserole, discard salt, and return petals to casserole; add 2 ounces of powdered orris root, 3 tablespoons brown sugar, and 3-4 ounces crushed spices. To strengthen flower scents, add 1 ounce of benzoin or 2 tablespoons brandy (optional). Store in casserole another 2 weeks, stirring several times a day to blend the fragrances. Use to fill small covered jars or to place in linen closets and drawers.

ROSE-LAVENDER POTPOURRI: Start with 10 ounces each of rose petals and lavender and add 5 ounces of sweet rose leaves and 2 ounces of ground orris root. Combine with 3/4 ounce of cinnamon bark broken fine, 1/2 ounce each of allspice and clove, and 6 drops of oil of tonka (or 10 beans).

BAY ROSE POTPOURRI: To 3 quarts rose petals add 12 torn bay leaves, 2 handfuls of lavender flowers and 1 handful each of orange blossoms, violets, and clove carnations. Mix in 2 ounces of orris root, 1 ounce of pounded nutmeg, 1/4 ounce each of cinnamon and ground clove and sprinkle with 1/2 ounce of oil of neroli.

SPICE POTPOURRI: Mix 1 quart rose petals with 1/2 pint lavender flowers, a teaspoon anise seed, 1 tablespoon of cloves, nutmeg and cinnamon mixed together and crushed, 1 tablespoon of crushed benzoin and 5 drops of oils of jasmine, rose geranium, patchouli, and rosemary.

LAVENDERWOOD POTPOURRI: Use 16 ounces lavender flowers combined with 2 ounces sweet woodruff, 1/2 ounces each of moss and thyme, 8 ounces of slivered orange peel, 4 ounces of benzoin and several handfuls of other available flowers. Finish off with 1/4 ounce of clove and anise combined.

ROSEMARY POTPOURRI: To 1 quart rose petals add 2 pints crushed lemon verbena leaves, 1 pint of rose geranium leaves, and 1 pint rosemary, slightly crushed, 1 tablespoon dried and crushed orange peel, 2 tablespoons benzoin and orris root mixed, a small quantity of finely cut angelica root, and a small quantity of mixed cinnamon, nutmeg, and sliced ginger root. Over this mixture sprinkle 6 drops each of oils of tonka, rosemary, and neroli.

PEPPERMINT POTPOURRI: To 1 pint each of peppermint leaves, thyme, and lavender flowers add 1 tablespoon crushed coriander, cloves, and nutmeg combined, 2 tablespoons crushed caraway seeds, and a tablespoon of crushed benzoin.

JASMINE POTPOURRI: To 8 ounces jasmine flowers add 4 ounces each of calamus, geranium leaves, and orange blossoms. Mix in 2 ounces each of cassia and benzoin sprinkled with 1 ounce of vanilla.

SACHET
A sachet is a small bag containing perfumed powder, used to scent clothes, linens, or notepapers. To make a sachet, dry the ingredients as for dry potpourri. All petals and leaves must be quite crisp, otherwise they may mildew. Sachets can be made from dry potpourri or they can be made from scratch with small quantities of flower materials.
PATCHOULI SACHET: Mix together 8 ounces each vetiver root, rose (or geranium) leaves, 6 ounces patchouli leaves, and 5 ounces ground mace. This scent goes well with woolens and blankets.
FLORIDA SACHET: To 8 ounces orange flowers add 3 ounces ground coriander seeds, 4 ounces fresh or 6 ounces dried mint leaves, 1 ounce benzoin, 2 ounces vetiver root, 2 ounces calamus, and 1 ounce sakmoss. Sprinkle with 4 drops neroli oil and let age, checking occasionally to see if it's fruity enough.
OAKASIA SACHET: Combine 2 ounces oakmoss, santal or ground sandalwood (white), and 2 ounces orris root. To this add 1 ounce ground tonka bean or 4 drops oil of tonka, 2 ounces dried and ground lemon peel, and 4 ounces acacia flowers.
ORANGE-ROSE SACHET: To 8 ounces orange and rose blossoms add 2 ounces each of finely ground magnolia flowers and bitter orange peel (you may have to substitute 2 drops of magnolia oil). Add 4 ounces finely ground santal or sandalwood and moisten with 4 drops oil of vanilla and a small vanilla bean crushed fine.
SWEET BAG FOR LINEN: Take a pound of orris roots, a pound of sweet calamus, a pound of cypress roots, a pound of dried lemon peel, a pound of dried orange peel, and a pound of dried roses. Make all of these into a gross powder. Then take 4 ounces coriander seeds, 1-1/2 ounce nutmeg, and 1 ounce cloves; make these into a fine powder and mix with the other. Add musk and amber grease; then take 4 large handfuls lavender flowers, a handful of sweet marjoram, a handful of orange leaves, a handful of young walnut leaves—all dried—and mix together with some bits of cotton perfumed with essences. Put up in silk bags to lay with your linen.
SACHET BASE: You can make this base and add oils to it as you like. To 4 ounces ground orris root add 4 ounces ground sandalwood, 1 ounce ground cedar, and 1 ounce lavender flowers. Mix in 1-1/2 ounces ground tonka bean, 2/3 ounce benzoin, and 1 teaspoon ground cloves. Sprinkle over this 1/4 ounce tincture of musk. The entire mixture should be ground together into a fine powder and stored for 2 weeks in a crock. It can be scented with almost any oil.
SUPPLIES: If there are no herb shops in your area, or if you are unable to find some item, contact one or more of the following firms for a catalog from which you may order by mail.

Aphrodisia
28 Carmine Street
New York, N.Y. 10014

Caswell-Massey Co. Ltd.
518 Lexington Avenue
New York, N.Y. 10017

Fioretti
1472 Lexington Avenue
New York, N.Y. 10028

Herb Products Co.
11013 Magnolia
North Hollywood, Calif.

Kiehl Pharmacy
1093 Third Avenue
New York, N.Y. 10021

Penn Herb Co.
603 North Second Street
Philadelphia, Pa. 19123

16 Decorations for a Colonial Christmas

This section was developed through the author's attendance at many delightful Williamsburg Christmas decoration workshops conducted at Great Falls National Park, Virginia. Special thanks are due the National Park Service and Mrs. Colleen Spicka, Park Specialist.

Colonial Christmases were characterized by decorations made from greens, fruits, flowers, and other natural materials—Santa Claus and Christmas trees had not yet appeared on the scene. Gifts were tokens of appreciation given to faithful servants on St. Steven's day, the day after Christmas; occasionally children received New Year's remembrances.

Christmas was a festive time then as now, full of feasts, family reunions, weddings, traveling theatre, and other entertainments—a time of great conviviality!

Here are some suggestions for celebrating Christmas—like it was.

APPLE FAN

AGE GROUP: Family or group project

MATERIALS: Piece of plywood; saw; finishing nails (about 3 inches long); hammer; magnolia leaves; antifreeze or other leaf preservative; 2-3 dozen apples (red); 1 pineapple; 2 screw eyes; pencil

DIRECTIONS: Cut plywood the width of front door, then cut into a semi-circle. Draw radiating pencil lines from the middle bottom point to the outer edges of the fan. Secure the screw eyes used for hanging fan. Hammer the nails in concentric half-circles (see illustration). These nails will hold first the magnolia leaves, then the apples, and then the pineapple on the fan. Soak the magnolia stems in leaf preservative—1 part antifreeze to 3 parts water will do—for about 8 hours. Pull the magnolia leaves from the stems, clean leaves, and shine with mayonnaise. Starting at the outside (curved) edge of the fan, push the leaves, shiny side up, onto the nails, overlapping them. Then start a slightly smaller half-circle overlapping the first row. Continue until the board is covered. Push the pineapple onto the nails in the center, then cover the rest of the nails with the red apples.

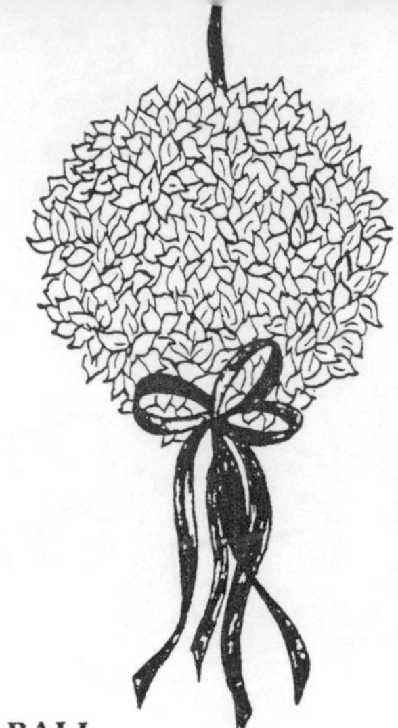

APPLE CONE
AGE GROUP: 9 or older
MATERIALS: 4x4-inch scraps of lumber, about 14 inches long (or a 6-inch diameter log); 48 finishing nails (about 3 inches long); magnolia leaves; 1 pineapple; hammer; enough small, shiny apples to cover all 4 sides of cone
DIRECTIONS: Hammer nails into all four sides of lumber, as shown. Be sure nails are secure; however, leave sufficient exposed nail for fastening leaves and fruit. Pull magnolia leaves from stems and attach as in Apple Fan, above. Then start at the top and completely cover the 4 by 4 with overlapping leaves. Push the pineapple in place on top, then cover cone with touching apples.

KISSING BALL
AGE GROUP: 7 or older
MATERIALS: Chicken wire, 12 by 18 inches; wire; wire cutters; ribbon; greens—boxwood, hedging, pine, holly, etc.; sleigh bells or mistletoe
DIRECTIONS: Form a ball with the chicken wire, roughly 4 inches in diameter, overlapping edges and bending to shape. Secure a piece of wire to the ball to hang. Push small pieces of greens into the chicken wire, completely covering the ball. Be sure the ball is full, with no bare spots. Then wrap the hanging wire with ribbon. Attach sleigh bells or mistletoe to bottom of ball; add ribbon strips to bottom.

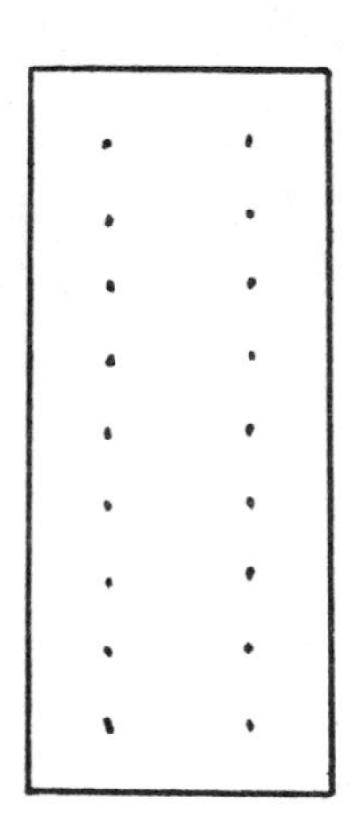

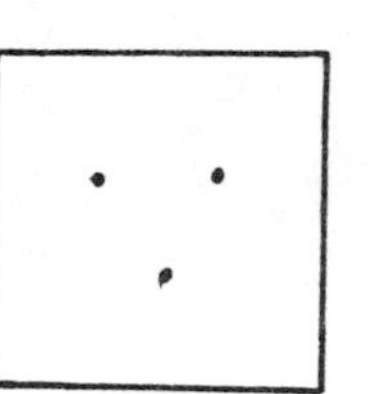

MINI-TREE

AGE GROUP: 7 or older

MATERIALS: 12- to 18-inch width chicken wire, about 24 inches long; red or white pine, or cedar; decorations (ribbon bows, cranberries, florist picks, etc.)

DIRECTIONS: Shape the chicken wire into a cone. Bend "raw" edges back into the cone to secure. Then, beginning at the base, push greens into the chicken wire holes, with needles going upwards. Balance the greens as you build upward; be sure tree is full and symmetrical. Add decorations. Spray greens with preservative to extend life of tree.

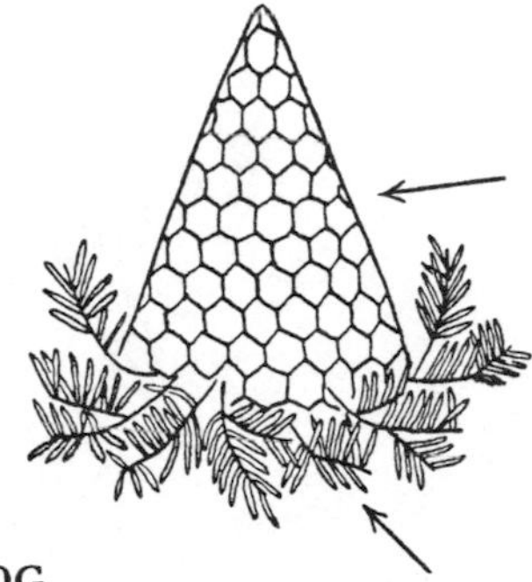

YULE LOG

AGE GROUP: 9 or older

MATERIALS: Pine cones; greens; penny finishing nails (about 3 inches long); a log roughly 8 inches in diameter and 18 inches long; white glue; wire (about 24 gauge size); hammer; wire cutters; old piece of rug or matting for bottom of log

DIRECTIONS: Hammer nails about every 3 inches over bark covering sides of log. Place pine cones in spaces between the nails. Wind wire around top of nails to form a grid so that pine cones won't dislodge easily. Then tuck small pieces of greens between nails, cones and wire. If holly or pyracantha-type berries are available, place a sprig here and there.

STRAW WREATH

AGE GROUP: Family or recreation group project.

MATERIALS: Florist's wreath frame of whatever size you wish; straw (not hay); fishing line (leave on reel)

DIRECTIONS: Place straw in the "V" groove of the wreath and secure by wrapping the fishing line around the straw to secure in place; keep adding straw and wrapping with the line. Make straw full and symmetrical.

VARIATION: You will need an abandoned bird's nest, two artificial buds, some plaid ribbon (1-1/2 to 3-inches wide); velvet ribbon (2-1/2 to 3 inches wide); *large* wreath pins; 3-inch wide velvet wired ribbon for large bow. Cut 8 pieces of velvet ribbon, each about 7-1/2 inches to 8 inches long. Cut an equal number of plaid ribbons of same length to top the velvet ribbon. Make a large, full bow from the wired velvet ribbon. Attach wire to the bow and attach to bottom of wreath. Wire nest and buds as in illustration.

VARIATION: Add holly and bright berries to basic straw wreath.

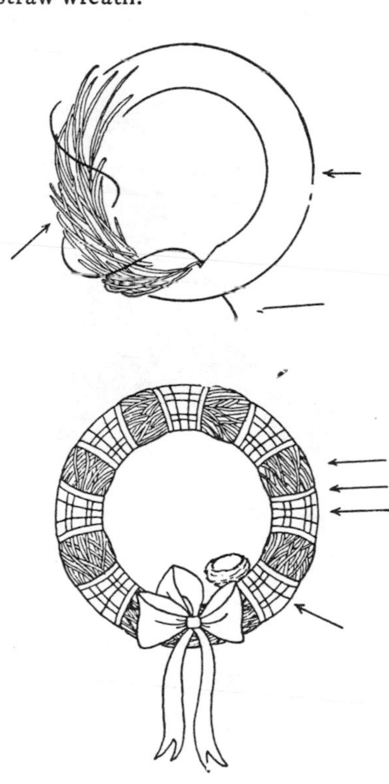

DELLA ROBBIA WREATH

AGE GROUP: Family or group project.

MATERIALS: 1 basic straw wreath or some other wreath form; 1 roll green plastic wrap (from florist); large package of *large* wreath pins; florist picks; greens; fresh fruits (lemons, crabapples, limes, tangerines, oranges, grapes, pears, apples—use local fruits if possible)

DIRECTIONS: Wrap the basic wreath with plastic green wrap, overlapping a bit; secure with a couple of wreath pins. Then attach small pieces of greens to the wreath with wreath pins. Keep the greenery going in the same direction and cover the sides and top of the wreath with greens. Using florist's picks secure the fruits to the greenery-covered wreath.

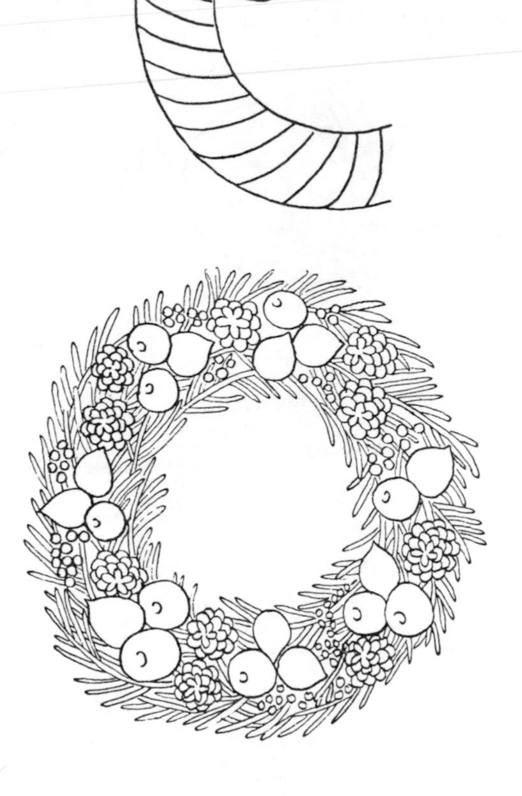

GARLAND

AGE GROUP: 7 or older—group project.

MATERIALS: 24-gauge wire on spool; greens; pruning shears; decorations (optional)

DIRECTIONS: Starting at one end keep the greenery going in the same direction; bend one branch to the next with the wire. There is no supporting foundation—just greens and wire. Keep the garland evenly full. Decorate, if desired, with fruits, berries, ribbons, etc.

FRUIT SWAG

AGE GROUP: 6 or older—group project

MATERIALS: Fresh fruit of various colors; nuts; 3 feet of strong chain; fine wire; 1-inch eye screws; ribbon; pine cones

DIRECTIONS: Suspend chain at a convenient height. Secure fruit to the chain with fine wire. To attach stemmed fruit, twist the wire around each stem and thread it through the chain links. For unstemmed fruit, insert screw eyes through the fruit rind only. Tuck sprigs of greenery and some pine cones between the fruit. Tie a satin ribbon to the top of the chain.

Victuals

Take a look at the colonial bill of fare. How were foods seasoned, prepared and cooked? Why not share this opportunity with your family and friends to experience the victuals of the late eighteenth century America?

17 Authentic Foods and Recipes

Special thanks are due Dave Murphy, farm manager at Turkey Run Farm, a replica of an 18th-century farm administered by the National Park Service in Langley, Virginia. His assistance in preparing this chapter was valuable.

To better understand colonial life, it is good to have some knowledge of young America's victuals, from the fare of the well-to-do merchant in Philadelphia to that of a modest farmer from backwoods Kentucky. What a delightful way to celebrate the Bicentennial—by cooking and eating dishes and foods that were enjoyed 200 years ago . . . like it was!

The colonial cook was extremely important. She had to farm, chop wood, tend fires, "put food by" (preserve), and sometimes help hunt and trap game. Small game, seasonal vegetables, wild berries, and large amounts of corn meal formed the staple diet of the masses. Stored food reflected what was locally available; oranges and lemons were not trucked to Connecticut from Florida or California. Geography thus played a central role in determining what the colonists ate; their diet was not nearly as varied as ours is today. There were also ethnic influences, with English or German settlers bringing their traditional dishes and recipes with them. Gradually these disparate foods were pooled, but at the same time more and more varieties of foods were developed and grown, resulting in ever-increasing diversity.

MEATS: Deer, squirrel, and rabbit were probably the most common wild game eaten by the early settlers. Some ate beaver (which tends to be tough and dry), polecat (sweet), raccoon (better than mutton), wildcat (like veal), buffalo, wild bear (good flavor), and rattlesnakes (roasted by Indians).

Domesticated livestock filled in the gaps left by depletion of wild animals.

FOWL: Wild falcons, hawks, eagles, buzzards, songbirds, water fowl, turkeys—almost anything that flew was hunted and eaten. Domesticated chicken, geese, and ducks with their eggs were welcome additions to the colonists' fare.

SEAFOOD: From the inland waters and coast people harvested cod, clams, eels, sturgeon, salmon, shad, lampreys, porpoise, mantee, alligators (in the South), whale, sea turtles and terrapin, frogs, lobsters, oysters, scallops, cockles, and mussels.

Preservation of meat, fowl, or seafood was a problem. Some solutions included smoking, pickling, salting, and eating quickly what had been killed.

BREADS: Part of the everyday diet, breads were popular and varied. When the finer grains ran low (as they often did), cornmeal mixes, rice, and dried pumpkin and potato flours were made into muffins and fritters. The names of many foods are derived directly from the ingredients or method of preparation, e.g., hoe cakes (baked in fireplace on the flat end of a hoe), ash cakes (wrapped in cabbage leaves and baked in the fireplace ashes), scratch backs (prepared from thick corn pudding that was hard and uneven and scratched the back of the eater's mouth), bannock cake (baked on a bannock board), and Maryland beaten biscuits (batter was beaten with a heavy ax handle for an hour before cooking). Wheat flour was a basic ingredient for loaf breads, biscuits, muffins, and rusk. Light resin yeast breads did not become popular until the 1770's.

VEGETABLES: Indian corn, or maize, grew abundantly and required little attention. The colonists adopted the agricultural practices of their Indian neighbors and planted corn, pumpkins, and beans at the same time and together. During the autumn, corn was eaten fresh—boiled or roasted on the cob; a succotash stew of beans and corn was popular. Most corn was ground into meal. The most popular corn concoctions were hasty pudding (sometimes called loblolly); quickly cooked gruel of corn meal boiled in equal parts with milk or water; Indian pudding, a more liquified version of hasty pudding with spices; suppawn, a thick mixture of corn meal and milk, eaten hot or cold from the pot or sliced and fried; mush, a watery type of suppawn eaten with sweetened fruit or molasses; samp porridge, an Indian goulash made of corn meal cooked for three days with meats and vegetables which could be removed from the pot in one solid chunk; rockahominy, corn meal finely powdered and dried—used for quick energy on the trail.

Pumpkins, squash, peas, lentils, baked beans, sweet potatoes, rice, and jerusalem artichokes were the most common vegetables consumed. Many vegetables imported from England flourished, such as cabbages, parsnips, carrots, beets, cauliflower, asparagus, turnips, spinach, and endive. Tomatoes were eaten as early as 1710 but were not popular for another hundred years as they were thought to be a member of the poisonous nightshade family. Wild onions were eaten raw, roasted, or used for flavoring stews. Mixed greens and vegetable salads, topped with oil and vinegar dressings, were well known. While meat was the staple of the white colonists, vegetables and grains formed the bulk of the diet of American slaves.

FRUITS: The Spanish settlers in Florida cultivated both imported and indigenous fruits—figs guavas, grapes, lemons, limes, citrons, shaddock and plantains (a form of banana). In the North, apples and peach orchards were planted. Wild berries were found virtually everywhere. Many of these were used for winemaking; other alcoholic drinks were produced from pears, peaches, currants, and shrub roots. Tree nuts were an important source of food.

SWEETENINGS: White processed sugar was expensive, and for the most part was used for special occasions. Molasses was a low-cost by-product of the sugar refining process and was used widely. Honey could be gathered, but the supply was limited and the long hours spent in searching for it were a drawback. Adapting Indian methods, colonists tapped sap-producing trees such as the sugar maple, mostly in the North.

DESSERTS: As sugar and syrups became more plentiful, confections began to replace fruits and preserved fruit as the chief satisfiers of the colonial sweet tooth. Flummery, a soft cream custard, thickened by gelatin and then topped with ground nuts, syrups and fruit preserves; syllabub, curdled cream with lemon, wine and sugar whipped to a thick froth; tasty puddings; whitespots, bread pudding baked in pastry shells; wild berry or fruit tarts and pies; deep-dish cobblers; and cakes were all popular desserts in colonial times. The most typical candies included roots and seeds of various plants dried and coated with sugar, and simple mixtures of sugar boiled with water and flavored with spices. Peppermint drops and horehound sweets were also popular.

BEVERAGES: Chocolate was a popular drink for all ages. Coffee and tea tastes were unpredictable. Substitutes for these were popular, though not as palatable. Excessive is probably the best way to describe the consumption of alcoholic drinks, from our point of view. Colonists drank for many reasons—sanitary conditions, especially in the more densely populated areas, made water hazardous to the health, and ciders, brews, and wine made the sometimes harsh colonial life more tolerable. Hard cider was probably the most popular drink, and beer was readily available. Domestic wines were made for the most part by the more affluent colonists, as sugar was an expensive commodity.

ONE POT MEALS

These were cooked in brass or iron kettles. Each day the stew was boiled and could be heated and reheated over a considerable length of time, especially in winter. These dishes were easier to prepare than meals comprised of several courses, which required additional utensils. Following are some delicious and authentic one pot meals.

MULLIGAN STEW (serves 12)

1-1/2 pounds beef, cut in pieces
1-1/2 pounds lamb, cut in pieces
3 fistfuls flour
3 quarts boiling water
1 inch square of butter
3 carrots thinly sliced
2 parsnips thinly sliced
1 large onion, diced
2 green peppers, diced
2 sticks celery, diced
8 potatoes, diced
salt and pepper
paprika

Wash, dry, season, and roll meat in two fistfuls of flour. Put butter and meat in bottom of a pot and sear meat on all sides. Add boiling water and prepared vegetables. Simmer for about two hours. Thicken the stew with the remainder of the flour, mixed in a little cold water.

POET AND PEASANT (serves 12)

1/3 C butter, fat or oil
8 onions
10 large tart apples, sliced
1-1/2 cup water
1 teaspoon salt

Heat the fat in a frying pan and slice the onions into it. Cook slowly until nearly tender; then add the apples, water, and salt. Cover and cook until the apples are soft. Remove the cover and fry until the water is all gone, and the onions and apples are a light brown color.

BRUNSWICK STEW

This famous Southern dish can be varied many ways. It is often made in large quantities for an out-of-doors get-together and can be made of squirrel and rabbit as well as stewing chicken. Sometimes pieces of stewing beef and pork spareribs are cooked with the chicken, and other vegetables are added, such as green beans, okra, diced potatoes and peas. Modern versions include tomatoes, which were not eaten by early colonists.

(serves 6-8)

1 stewing chicken cut in pieces
salt
1 onion, sliced thin
1 cup green lima beans
3 potatoes, sliced thin
1 tablespoon sugar
pepper
1/2 cup dried corn soaked in 1 cup of boiling water or
1 cup fresh corn
1/4 pound butter

Cover the chicken with boiling water. Cover and simmer until tender (about 1-1/2 hours). Add 2 tsp salt after 45 minutes. Take out the pieces of chicken, remove the bones and cut the meat in 1 inch pieces. Put back in the pot and add onion, lima beans, potatoes, sugar, and salt and pepper to taste. Cook until the beans and potatoes are tender. Add the corn, any other vegetables desired, and the butter. Cook 5 minutes.

BOSTON BAKED BEANS (serves 6-8)

1 pound dried navy or pea beans
1/2 pound salt pork (without rind)
1 medium onion, sliced (optional)
1/4 cup brown sugar, packed
3 tablespoons molasses
1 teaspoon salt
1/4 teaspoon dry mustard
1/8 teaspoon pepper

Place beans in a large pan and cover with water. Heat to boiling; boil 2 minutes. Remove from heat and let stand 1 hour. Add water, if necessary, to cover beans; simmer uncovered 50 minutes or until tender. Be sure not to boil or the beans will burst. Drain beans, reserving liquid.

Cut salt pork into several pieces; layer with beans and onions in bean pot (if cooked in oven) or Dutch oven. Stir together remaining ingredients with one cup of the reserved liquid; pour over beans. Add enough of the reserved liquid to almost cover beans. Cover and bake slowly in a warm oven (150°) or bake in low coals for 6 to 8 hours. Uncover during the last hour of cooking to "brown up" the meat.

Serve with brown bread.

OLD-FASHIONED BEEF STEW

Use beef from the rump, tip or shank. Allow 1/4 to 1/2 pounds of meat per person. Remove most of the fat and all of the gristle. If available, retain a small piece of cracked bone to cook with the meat. Cut the meat into 1-1/2 inch cubes. Sprinkle with salt and pepper and roll in flour. Melt some of the fat from the meat in the stew pot. Brown the meat thoroughly in the fat to a deep rich color. For added flavor cook a slice or two of onion with the meat.

Cover with stock (or boiling water), bring to a boil, cover and simmer until meat is fork tender (2-3 hours). Skim off any fat that rises to the surface. Season to taste with salt, pepper, thyme, or any seasonings desired.

Any vegetables that are desired and available can be added to the basic beef stew. These might include carrots, onions, potatoes, celery, parsnips, corn, peas, beans, or cauliflower. (Allow up to an hour cooking time for whole carrots or onions.) Mushrooms may be added too, as long as they are edible.

If a thicker stew is desired add more flour to the stew. This pot may be reused adding leftover vegetables or meats from other meals.

OLD-FASHIONED FISH CHOWDER

(serves 8 generously)

4 pounds cod or haddock, skinned and boned. Retain the head, tail, and backbone.
2 cups cold water
1-1/2 inch cube fat salt pork, diced
1 onion sliced thin
4 cups thinly sliced potatoes
2 cups boiling water
4 cups scalded milk or cream
1 tablespoon salt
1/8 teaspoon pepper
3 tablespoons butter

Put the head, tail and bone (broken in pieces) in a deep kettle and add cold water. Simmer slowly 10 minutes. Drain and save the liquid. Put the pork in a small frying pan. Cook slowly 5 minutes and add the onion. Cook until soft (about 5 minutes). Strain the fat into a deep pan and set the crisp scraps aside. Add the potatoes and boiling water to the kettle. Cook 5 minutes. Add the fish, cut in 2-inch pieces, and the liquid drained from the bones. Cover and simmer 10 minutes. Add the scraps of onion and pork. Add the milk, salt, pepper, and butter. Heat but do not boil.

CORN CHOWDER (serves 12)

12 slices fat bacon or salt pork
10 medium sized potatoes, diced
5 cups fresh (canned) corn or 2-1/2 cups dried corn soaked in 5 cups of water.
2 quarts liquid (water, stock, or milk)
salt and pepper

Cut the bacon or pork and onions very small. Fry in a kettle until brown, stirring frequently to prevent burning. Pour off extra grease, if necessary. Add diced potatoes, about 1/2 hour before time for serving. Cook until done. Just before the potatoes are done, add the corn. Season and add the liquid. If milk is used, add just prior to serving. Bring to boiling point, but do not boil.

This may serve as a basic chowder recipe; ham, fish, clams, or vegetables may be used in place of the corn. If fresh vegetables are used, it will be necessary to cook them longer.

DAIRY PRODUCTS

ICE CREAM

The dairy product with the most interesting history is ice cream. One of the earliest mentions of ice cream is in a letter written by a dinner guest of Governor Bladen of Maryland, which notes, "... we had a dessert no less curious; among the rarities of which it was compos'd was some fine ice cream which, with the strawberries and milk, eat most deliciously." From the beginning, ice cream has been America's favorite dessert. In the late 18th and early 19th centuries, however, only the elite could afford ice for freezing the cream. For a time, ice cream was a symbol of wealth and prosperity.

George Washington was a special patron of ice cream, and had two pewter ice cream pots for making it. He was especially pleased when Alexander Hamilton's wife served it at a dinner party in 1789. He was so fanatic about it that the records of a New York ice cream merchant show that Washington ran up a bill of $200 for ice cream in the summer of 1790.

Early methods required a lot of strength and time, as the mixture had to be beaten in a pot at the same time the pot was shaken up and down in a large pan of salt and ice. Modern methods are quicker and simpler. A hand-cranked ice cream freezer gives a feel for the colonial way of making this popular confection. This is how:

1. Scald and then chill can, cover, and dasher before using.
2. Fill can with mixture not more than 3/4 full.
3. Pack outside can with fine, evenly chopped ice and rock salt.
4. Use 3 parts ice to 1 part salt.
5. Turn crank slowly for first 5 minutes then quickly until it is hard to turn.
6. Keep adding salt and ice as needed. Drain off extra water.

PLAIN VANILLA ICE CREAM

1 pint hot milk
2 tablespoons flour
1 cup sugar
2 eggs separated
2 teaspoons vanilla
1 quart cream

Mix flour, sugar, and 1/8 teaspoon salt, adding milk gradually. Cook over hot water 10 minutes, stirring occasionally. Take from stove, and stir into the well-beaten egg yolks very gradually. Cook until the mixture coats the spoon. Cool, add cream, stiffly beaten egg whites and flavoring, strain and freeze in ice cream freezer.

PHILADELPHIA ICE CREAM

1 quart cream
1 cup sugar
1 teaspoon vanilla

Heat one cup of the cream, add sugar; cool; add flavoring and remaining cream. Freeze in ice cream freezer.

VARIATIONS:

Strawberry: Mash 2 cups of strawberries and incorporate them.

Coffee: Chill 1/2 cup of black unsweetened coffee and add it.

Banana: Pound four bananas with two tablespoons of strained lime juice and add.

Peach: Stew enough skinned peaches to make one cup; pound them to a pulp and add to Philadelphia cream.

HONEY ICE CREAM

Beat two egg yolks. Add 1/2 cup honey, 2 cups cream, 1 teaspoon vanilla, 1 cup nuts. Beat two egg whites until stiff and add to the above. Pour into the inner compartment of freezer. Crank until frozen.

GEORGE WASHINGTON CHERRY ICE CREAM

Prepare vanilla or Philadelphia ice cream.

When mixture is 3/4 frozen, add 1 cup chopped, drained marischino cherries. Finish freezing. Use the cherry juice as sauce.

CHOCOLATE ICE CREAM

Cook 2 ounces of grated chocolate (1/2 cup when grated) with 1 cup of white sugar and 3 tablespoons of rapidly boiling water; stir the while. Remove this from the fire and, while it cools, whip and add 1 quart of cream; also add 3 teaspoons of vanilla extract. Put into freezer. (Note: 1/2 pint of cream and 1-1/2 pints of whole milk may be substituted for the quart of cream.)

CHEESE

The basic tools for making cheese are cheesecloth and a bowl. Cheesecloth is a loosely woven material which allows the whey (liquid which is left as cheese forms) to drain while it holds the curd (the solid) as it dries. Cheesecloth can be purchased at hardware stores and in houseware departments. Use the bowl when draining cheese to catch the whey, which can be used later. Hang aging cheese in a cool place and store cheese in a cool place. Here are some simple cheese recipes:

COTTAGE CHEESE

Heat sour milk to wrist temperature. Strain through a diaper or cheesecloth. Mix salt with the curds.

HARD CHEESE

Heat one gallon milk to wrist temperature and add one crushed junket rennet tablet (available at grocery stores). When solid, salt and drain in cheesecloth. Age a few days, the longer the better.

CREAM CHEESE

Cover a wide shallow dish with cheesecloth and ladle cream into it. Let stand until thick (until it can be hung without cream running out).

MONKEY CHEESE

1/2 cup stale bread crumbs
1 cup milk
2 teaspoons butter
1/2 cup grated mild cheese
1 egg, beaten
cayenne, salt, powdered mustard

Soak crumbs fifteen minutes. Melt butter and add cheese. Stir until cheese melts. Add egg to crumbs and milk mixture and stir in seasonings (to taste). Add to cheese mixture and heat until smooth. Serve on toast.

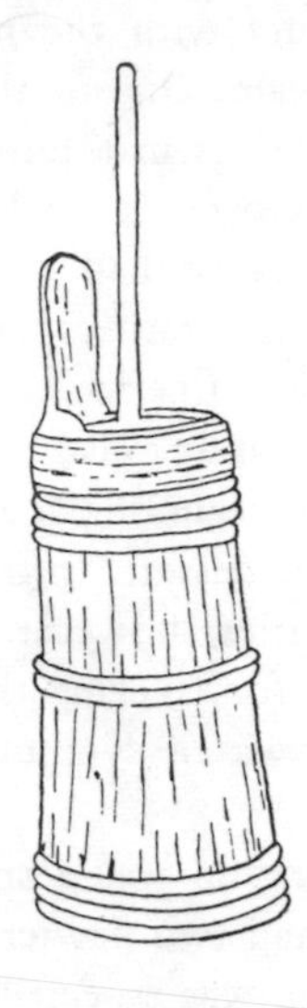

BUTTER

Everyone should have a chance to work a butter churn. By twisting and moving the paddle up and down for about an hour, cream turns to butter. After it has formed it can be molded by hand or by pressing it into a wooden or plastic box. If a standard churn cannot be found, substitutions can be easily made. Small churns which screw into one quart Mason jars are available. Some are electric; others can be manipulated by hand. Here is a recipe for making butter:

Let the milk stand 24 hours in hot summer and 48 hours in winter. Both the churn and the cream should be kept at temperatures 55-60 degrees F. The butter will come after 15 minutes of churning. Gather it together, work with a wooden paddle in wooden bowl and wash out buttermilk by pouring in very cold water until the water runs clear. For variety, churn in bits of fruit and tasty petals.

An even simpler method of making butter uses a jar: obtain 1 pint 40% butterfat cream. Put fresh cream in jar with a tight lid. Shake until yellow butterfat forms in center (about 20 minutes). Pour off buttermilk (which is sweet and delicious); press the butter to remove rest of milk and salt to taste. Makes 1/2 pound.

Butter may or may not be salted according to taste. For added interest, butter prints can be used to press designs into the butter. These can be purchased at most gourmet food stores or can be made by carving a raised pattern from a small block of wood. Butter should be stored in a cool place. It is best when used right away.

BREAD

In colonial America, cornbread was common, because corn was more plentiful than wheat. Cornbread was carried for sustenance when people travelled, so it was called journeycake. The word "journeycake" evolved to johnnycake.

Our nation has a fascinating breadmaking heritage, which resulted from a mixture of many nationalities. In colonial times, English and Scottish cookbooks were used; it was not until the 1770's that a cookbook was even printed in the United States. Several breads are unique to America, including Anadama Bread from New England.

To highlight the changes recipes have undergone, several have been reprinted as they appeared in early cookbooks. Others have been selected for their popularity during the colonial period. When more than one description is presented, they have been arranged chronologically so the last ones will be similar to breadmaking techniques in the 1970's. Only the recipes which are somewhat difficult to obtain are included. Variations of yeast and quick breads may be easily found in present-day cookbooks.

FRENCH BREAD

Take a quart of Flower, and put to it three spoonsfuls of ale-yeast, and an equal quantity of milk and water warm'd; about the bigniss of a Walnut of good butter, and a little Salt; make them pretty tight and drop them on Tin Plates, set them before the Fire to rise, and bake them in a quick oven, rasp them; some People put three Eggs, only one white, to this quantity, but I think Eggs make it tough, and not so short; but that as you please.

Receipts in Cookery (1719)

TO MAKE COMMON BISCUITS

Beat up six eggs, with a spoonful of rose-water and a spoonful of sack; then add a pound of fine powdered sugar, and a pound of flour; mix them into the eggs by degrees, and an ounce of corianderseeds; mix all well together, shape them on white thin paper, or tin moulds, in any form you please. Beat the white of an egg, with a feather rub them over, and dust fine sugar over them. Set them in an oven moderately heated, till they rise and come to a good colour, take them out; and when you have done with the oven, if you have no stove to dry them in, put them in the oven again, and let them stand all night to dry.

The Art of Cookery (1791)

TO MAKE FRENCH BISCUITS

Having a pair of clean scales ready, in one scale put three new-laid eggs, in the other scale put as much dried flour, an equal weight with the eggs, take out the flour, and as much fine powdered sugar; first beat the whites of the eggs up well with a whisk till they are of a fine froth; then whip in half an ounce of candied lemon-peel cut very thin and fine, and beat well; then by degrees whip in the flour and sugar, then slip in the yolks, and with a spoon temper it well together; then shape your biscuits on fine white paper with your spoon, and throw powdered sugar over them. Bake them in a moderate oven, not too hot, giving them a fine colour on the top. When they are baked, with a fine knife cut them off from the paper, and lay them in boxes for use.

The Art of Cookery (1791)

TO MAKE WHITE BREAD

To a gallon of the best flour put six ounces of butter, half a pint of good yest, a little salt, break two eggs into a bason, but leave out one of the whites, put a spoonful or two of water to them, and beat them up to a froth, and put them in the flour, have as much new milk as will wet it, make it just cream, and mix it up, lay a handful of flour and drive it about, holding one hand in the dough, and driving it with the other hand till it is quite light, then put it in your pan again, and put it near the fire, and cover it with a cloth, and let it stand an hour and a quarter; make your rolls ten minutes before you set them in the oven, and prick them with a fork; if they are the bigness of a French roll, three quarters of an hour will bake them.

The Experienced English Housekeeper (1796)

PATENT YEAST

Put a half a pound of fresh hops into a gallon of water, and boil it away to two quarts; then strain it, and make it a thin batter with flour; add half a pint of good yeast, and when well fermented, pour it in a bowl, and work in as much corn meal as will make it the consistency of biscuit dough; set it to rise, and when quite light, make it into little cakes, which must be dried in the shade, turning them very frequently; keep them securely from damp and dust. Persons who live in town, and can procure brewer's yeast, will save trouble by using it: take one quart of it, add a quart of water, and proceed as before directed.

The Virginia Housewife (1830)

ANADAMA BREAD

1/2 cup Indian meal
1 yeast cake, dissolved in 1/2 cup warm water
1/2 cup molasses
1/2 teaspoon salt
2 cups boiling water
2 tablespoons shortening
5 cups flour

Stir the Indian meal, very slowly, into the boiling water. When thoroughly mixed, add the shortening, molasses and salt. Cool. When lukewarm, add the dissolved yeast cake and the flour (enough to make a stiff dough). Knead well and keep in a warm place to rise more than double its bulk. Mould into loaves and let rise until light. Bake in a hot oven (400°F) for one hour.

SALLY LUNN

Put 1 yeast cake in 1 cup warm milk. Cream together 3 tablespoons shortening and 3 tablespoons sugar. Add 2 eggs and mix well. Sift in 3-1/2 cups flour to which 1-1/4 teaspoons salt has been added, alternately with the milk and yeast. Beat well. Let rise in a warm place (about double bulk). Knead lightly. Put into well greased Sally Lunn mold.* Let stand and rise again (double) and bake at 300 degrees F for 1 hour.

*A 3-1/2x10 inch ring mold or an angel food cake tin may be used.

QUICK SALLY LUNN

4 cups flour
4 eggs
1 pint milk
1 tablespoon sugar
2 tablespoons butter
1 teaspoon salt
2 teaspoons baking powder

Sift baking powder, salt, flour and 1 tablespoon of sugar. Beat eggs until very light. Add the milk to the flour, then the eggs and melted butter. Mix all together, stir well and bake in 425-degree F oven.

JOHNNYCAKE

2 cups bread flour
2 cups stone ground cornmeal
3 teaspoons of baking powder
1 package dry yeast, dissolved in 1/4 cup very warm water
4 tablespoons raw sugar
2 eggs
2 teaspoons salt
milk sufficient to make a very stiff batter (probably a little more than 1 cup)

Mix and bake at 350 degrees F for 20 minutes or until lightly browned.

VIRGINIA ASH CAKE

Add a teaspoonful of salt to a quart of sifted corn meal. Make up with water and knead. Make into round, flat cakes. Sweep a clean place on the hottest part of the hearth. Put the cake on it and cover it with the hot wood ashes.

Wash and wipe it dry, before eating it. Sometimes a cabbage leaf is placed under it, and one over it, before baking, in which case it need not be washed.

Housekeeping in Old Virginia (1879)

CORNMEAL PONES

Scald a quart of milk; stir in 1 pint of meal and 6 eggs, whites and yolks beaten separately, a little salt, 1 tablespoon flour, and 2 teaspoons baking powder. Bake in buttered white cups or small bowls and send to the table in the cups, so they may be hot to be turned out on to the plate and eaten with butter or syrup. Bake in a hot oven (425 degrees F) exactly 20 minutes.

HOE CAKE

2 cups corn meal
2 or 3 teaspoons salt
Boiling water

This old plantation dish was originally baked on a hoe over the fire. Up at the big house they added 1 cup of milk, 2 tablespoons butter and 1 teaspoon baking powder. In either case add enough scalding water to make a batter to form into cakes on a greased griddle, or bake in the oven on a greased sheet 30 minutes very slowly, at about 325 degrees F.

EARLY COLONIAL BREAD

1/2 cup yellow corn meal
1/3 cup brown sugar
1 tablespoon salt
2 cups boiling water
1/4 cup cooking oil
2 packages active dry yeast
1/2 cup lukewarm water
3/4 cup stirred whole wheat flour
1/2 cup stirred rye flour
4-1/4 to 4-1/2 cups sifted all purpose flour

Thoroughly combine the corn meal, brown sugar, salt, boiling water and oil. Let cool to lukewarm, about thirty minutes. Soften yeast in the 1/2 cup lukewarm water. Stir into the corn meal mixture. Add the whole wheat and rye flours; mix well. Stir in enough all-purpose flour to make a moderately stiff dough. Turn out on lightly floured surface and knead till smooth and elastic, 6 to 8 minutes. Place in greased bowl, turning once to grease surface. Cover and let rise in warm place till double, 50 to 60 minutes. Punch down; turn out on lightly floured surface and divide in half. Cover and let rest 10 min. Shape into two loaves and place in greased 9x5x3 inch loaf pans. Let rise again till almost double, about 30 min. Bake in 375 degrees F oven for 45 minutes or till done. (Cap with foil, loosely, after first 25 minutes if bread browns too rapidly.) Remove from pans. Cool on rack. Makes 2 loaves.

18 Fires for Heating and Cooking

OUR COLONIAL FOREBEARS had to rely on the fires they built inside and outside their homes for both heat and cooking. The fireplace was the focal point of the colonial home, and daily life centered there, especially during the cold winters. The common room, or kitchen, had a large fireplace for preparing meals and heating the room, which was usually fairly large. These large kitchen fireplaces were not a New England or colonial invention; they had descended from Plantagenet times in England. During the winters the fires were kept going almost continuously. The fire also served as the colonial family's primary source of light after sundown.

At the frontier, pioneers knew firebuilding to be an essential art for survival. Fires had to be built quickly, carefully (especially if there were hostile Indians about), and often under adverse and unfavorable conditions.

HOW TO START A FIRE: Matches were not invented until 1827; before that, flint and steel were widely used. A piece of steel, a flint (hard rock), and some tinder made from cotton or linen cloth, or dried powdered bark (white birch is probably best) were required. The tinder was sometimes heated until almost ready to burn, then kept in a tightly covered tinder box to keep it perfectly dry. When the fire was to be started, the tinder was placed on the ground and the flint struck against the steel—the flying sparks igniting the tinder. The back of a knife blade, an ax, or any piece of metal that produces sparks may be substituted for the steel. Actual flint rock is not absolutely necessary; quartz, agate, various pyrites and jasper are all good spark-producing rocks. The shredded bark of cedar or cypress trees is almost as good as white birch for natural tinder; even during a rain the inside of cedar bark usually remains dry. Other natural tinders are pine needles and small twigs (sometimes known as "squawwood"). Charred cloth is excellent as tinder because it catches easily and holds a spark (pioneers often carried charred cloth just for this purpose).

When starting a fire, make sure the sparks fly directly into the tinder. Then fan or blow it gently until it flames up. Place small pieces of wood or twigs on the fire and build it up progressively until it will take large pieces of wood, such as logs.

Another fire-starting technique is the friction method. Indians of various tribes used the "bow and drill" variation of this method very effectively. A pointed stick (the "drill") is twirled into a notch in a fireboard, grinding off fine powder. Heat from the friction of wood against wood causes the powder to smoulder as it drops through the notch onto tinder placed below it. Willow, elm, basswood, and cottonwood are some of the more common woods used for this purpose. Traditionally, the fireboard is about an inch thick though it can be a bit more or less. The board must be long enough so it can be held down firmly by kneeling or with one foot. To make one, have an edge of the board as smooth and straight as possible. Gouge out a hole in one side, about an inch in from the edge and about one-quarter-inch deep. Now cut a V-notch in the edge of the board, the "V" pointing toward the gouged place and cutting into the edge of it. Bevel the notch so it is wider at the bottom than at the top. It is into this notch and below the edge of the drill hole that the tinder will be placed and in which the powder, ground by friction and ignited by heat, will fall.

The simplest hand drill used by some Western Indians was a slender, rounded stick about 1-1/2 feet long, smoothed and tapered at the upper end. This hand drill is operated by kneeling on the end of the board and placing the palms together around the upper, tapered top end of the drill. The palms are then rubbed together, twirling the drill swiftly back and forth (reversing directions with each rub). The powdered wood ground off and heated eventually sets off smouldering as it falls into the tinder, and you can nurse a blaze to life. You'll then need kindling. Failure to split kindling is a primary cause of fire failures. Cedar is the best of all, but spruce, pine, and fir will also work well.

A "prayer stick" combines tinder and kindling. This is whittled so that long, curly shavings protrude from a stick in all directions. Two or three prayer sticks, heaped one on top of the other, will almost guarantee a brisk fire in short order.

Remember that, in general, evergreens are classified as "softwoods," and they are fast-burning, leave no coals, and will snap sparks all over a campsite. Hardwoods, or deciduous trees, burn slowly and create coals that glow for hours. A few species throw sparks initially but then settle down to steady burning. These include maple, beech, white oak, and hickory.

To start a fire under wet conditions, break open standing dry wood or gather small twigs of evergreens under spreading branches. A prayer stick cut from dry wood is especially good here. Try to start the fire under a large, fallen tree if possible. Dry fuel can often be found under big, upturned logs, shelving rocks, and similar natural shelters. Also look for dead softwood trees that lean to the south; the wood and bark of the underside will be dry. Snow presents special problems. Make a platform of logs so the fire will not melt the snow and sink out of sight. The wood, because of the dampness and cold, will remain almost fireproof for a few hours and will then burn reluctantly once it thaws.

TEE PEE FIRE. For a noonday lunch, or any other quick meal, a large fire is not needed. Gather an armful of dry, sound twigs and kindling and stand these in a tripod. Around them build a small conical wigwam of the bigger sticks, standing each on end and slanting toward the common center.

LOG CABIN FIRE. First get in plenty of wood and kindling and find two large, flat rocks or several small ones of even height. On these lay two 4-foot logs, parallel and several inches apart, as rests for pots. Arrange the kindling between and under them, with small and large sticks criss-crossed on top. Then light it and let the wood burn down to coals for an even-heated fire.

FIRE IN A TRENCH. In time of drought, when everything is tinder-dry, or in windy weather, build the fire in a trench. This is the best method too if fuel is scarce and you must depend on brushwood, as a trench conserves heat. Dig the trench in line with the prevailing wind—the point is to get a good draft. Make the windward end somewhat wider than the rest and deeper, sloping the trench upward to the far end. Line the sides with flat rocks, if available; they hold the heat and keep the sides from caving in.

HUNTER'S FIRE. Cut two hardwood logs not less than a foot thick and about 6 inches long. Lay these side by side, about a foot apart at one end and 6 or 8 inches at the other. Across them lay short green sticks as supports, and on these build a criss-cross pile of dry wood and set fire to it. The upper layers of wood will soon burn to coals which will drop between the logs and set them blazing.

WINTER CAMPFIRE. Designed to keep you warm at night. If there is a big, flat-faced rock or ledge on the campsite, take advantage of it by building your fire against it with the tent in front. Or build a wall of rocks for a fire-back. The fire-back reflects the heat forward into the tent, conducts the smoke upward, and serves as a windbreak in front of camp, so the higher it is—within reason—the better. The fire-back should not be more than 5 feet from the tent front; with a small, well-tended fire, it need not be more than 4 feet.

19 Growing, Cooking and Decorating with Herbs

GROWING, HARVESTING, AND USING HERBS can be immensely satisfying. You need only minimal growing space—a few pots or a sunny window sill. Herbs are attractive plants, they smell good, and they add tantalizing flavor to your cooking. Herbs make fine gifts, or they can even provide a chance to make some extra money for a worthwhile cause. Most colonial housewives actively cultivated herb gardens. Why don't you?

Early American housewives lived in close association with nature. They valued herbs for culinary, medicinal, and aromatic values. Most housewives probably grew only a few basic herbs in their individual gardens, such as mint, sage, parsley, thyme, and marjoram.

The major expense in establishing a modern herb garden is a few packets of seed or a few baby plants. Start with five or six hardy perennials, such as lemon balm, sage, and thyme. If growing them indoors in containers, mix 2 parts sterilized potting soil and 1 part coarse sand or perllite. Add 1 cup of ground limestone to one bushel of soil (or 1 teaspoon to a 5-inch pot) to insure sweetness. Place at least an inch of gravel in the bottom of the pot to allow drainage.

If planting outdoors, start with a small plot, perhaps 4 by 16 feet. Allow 2 square feet for each herb. Or, set aside a space in your regular vegetable garden for herbs. Choose a sunny location, as most herbs require full sun to thrive. The soil should be slightly alkaline and well drained. If your soil tends to be clayey, work in some sand and organic materials such as compost or peatmoss.

Most herbs grow well in dry soil, but during a prolonged dry spell some watering would be advisable, especially for early seedlings. The indoor gardener will need to pay careful attention to the water needs of each plant. Misting with an atomizer will provide welcome humidity—herbs like humidity but not soggy roots. Rotate your pots frequently so all sides get roughly equal amounts of sun—a south or west window is almost essential.

Seeds for annual herbs such as chervil, dill, parsley, and summer savory can be sowed directly into the outdoor garden in early spring. Parsley, although a biennial, is best treated as an annual because in the second growing season it goes to seed. Perennials are winter-hardy, except for marjoram and rosemary.

In harvesting herbs, don't injure the plant's growth by pulling off too many leaves from one stem or section of the plant. When the plants are large and full, cut sprigs from the ends of the stems—this is called pinching. It also stimulates new growth, causing the plant to become fuller and bushier.

To dry and store herbs, gather when they contain their maximum amounts of oils—flowers in summer, leaves and bark in spring, roots in spring and fall. Clean carefully before drying. Dry in quick oven (200 degrees) for several hours, outdoors on a screen for 3-4 days, or indoors on a screen in a warm room or attic. Store crushed or whole leaves in tightly covered jars. Drying roots takes more time: wash, slice or split large bulbs, spread on screen or pan and allow plenty of time. When thoroughly dry, store in air-tight containers. Gather seeds and spread on screen or pan covered with thin cloth or paper; turn frequently. When completely dry, store in covered bottles.

HINTS FOR FLAVORING WITH HERBS:

- Use culinary herbs as *additional* seasoning with usual amounts of salt, pepper, etc.
- Use a *small* amount of one or more herbs to enhance the flavor of the food.
- Taste and experiment until you are familiar with an herb's action.
- Heat releases herb oils quickly; cold does not. In cold juices, cheese, etc., herbs should be pre-soaked or added several hours before serving. In hot soups or stews, herbs are added about 30 minutes before cooking ends.
- Always keep herbs in tightly covered containers and in cool place.

THE BOUQUET GARNI

When using fresh herbs, you may wish to make a bouquet of the sprigs and tie them together with a string or in a cheesecloth bag so they can be removed when the food is cooked. A basic bouquet consists of 2 sprigs parsley, 1 sprig marjoram, 1 sprig basil, and 1 sprig thyme. There are many variations; experiment on your own. Take a bouquet to a sick friend, or put one in your next pot of homemade soup.

HERBS IN FLOWER ARRANGEMENTS

Perhaps no other plants make more satisfactory or beautiful arrangements than herbs. Arrangements can be displayed in a low, circular container, such as an ivy ring.

Fern leaf tansy has a lovely, dark, green, textured leaf resembling an ostrich plume. Perilla has a deep, red color; arrange in a vase with pink snapdragons or any other pink flower which blends well with this. Purple basil has a dark brown color with purple tinges and is also lovely with pink or lavender—its aroma is delightful. Most refreshing of all are the mints, used with any combination of flowers. They stand perky and fragrant in water for over a week.

When it comes to the grey herbs, many can be used to great advantage for looks and fragrance. Southernwood, a hardy perennial, is a tall, soft, feathery grey plant that combines well with any color. Artemesia silver mound, also a perennial, is just what its name implies: a silvery, very soft, feathery plant. A cool-appearing arrangement for a hot day can be made by using the dark green fern leaf tansy laid flat around the edge of a low dish, and filling the center with the soft, grey down of the artemesia silver mound.

Lemon balm, a hardy perennial, has a small, round, light green leaf which lends itself attractively to small arrangements.

ON SPECIFIC HERBS

BASIL is a pretty plant with bright green leaves and spikes of white flowers. It is an annual, 1 to 2 feet high. Regular pruning will insure a compact, bushy plant. Keep the flower spikes cut or the plant will set seed and die.

CHIVES are dainty members of the onion family. They have grey-green spikey leaves and clusters of light purple flowers 10 to 12 inches high. Perennial. Uses: Seasoning for salads, omelets and dishes that need a mild onion flavor. A member of the classic French "fines herbes." Cut the leaves at ground level as needed. Bunches of leaves can be chopped finely and frozen.

DILL has dark green, finely cut foliage on a branching single stalk. It has flat flower heads of greeny-white flowers followed by handsome seed heads. 2 to 3 feet high. Annual. Dill is most often used with fish. It is a favorite in the Scandinavian countries. The seeds are used to flavor pickles. Dill can be frozen if you pull the young plants when they are six to eight inches tall. Wrap tightly in a plastic bag and chop as needed. Seeds can be collected and stored.

The MINT family are vigorous growers that spread everywhere. The leaves are rich, green in color and give off a spicy fragrant scent. 2 to 3 feet high. Perennial. Mints make delicious tea and are most often used to flavor black tea and other beverages. They are also used for flavoring desserts, candy and jellies. Pick fresh leaves or leafy stems for flavoring. Leafy stems can be dried and stored for winter use.

PARSLEY'S rich green curled leaves make a good addition to your cooking pot and the garden. Italian parsley has a richer flavor and lighter green flat leaf. 10 to 12 inches high. Biennial. Parsley is most commonly used as a garnish but don't let it deck your plate. Chop fresh parsley generously into soups, salads, rice, and vegetables. This is a member of the French "fines herbes."

ROSEMARY is a woody perennial. The narrow dark green leaves are leathery and older plants that have ideal growing conditions have light blue flowers. 1 to 3 feet high. Perennial. The leaves have a rich spicy fragrance and flavor. The pungent flavor makes rosemary a good compliment to meat and stuffings. Sprigs can be cut and dried for winter use.

SAGE is a woody shrub-like herb. The leaves are oblong grey-green with a pebbly texture. The lavender blue flowers grow on spikes. 2 to 3 feet high. Perennial. Sage is a good complement for roasted meats, poultry stuffings and sausage.

SUMMER SAVORY has small bronzy-green leaves and white or lavender flowers. 18 inches high. Annual. The spicy flavor of summer savory is a great addition to bean salad. It is often used to season meat dishes and stuffing. Needless to say, it is good right from the garden. Cut young leaves and hang in a dark airy place to dry. Remove the leaves from the stems and store.

MARJORAM is a pungently fragrant herb with small velvet oval gray-green leaves and tiny white flowers. 8 to 12 inches high. Perennial. Marjoram is a good addition to eggs, sauces, soups, and stuffings. Use the fresh leaves and cut the leafy stems at flowering time and dry.

French TARRAGON has narrow twisted green leaves on many branches. Insist on French tarragon plants as the tarragon seed is not flavorful. 2 feet high. Perennial. Tarragon has a dominating flavor that is used in vinegars and salads. It is best to use tarragon fresh because the flavor changes when dry. Tarragon is a member of the "fines herbes."

There are many varieties of THYME with a wide range of fragrance and foliage color. French thyme has tiny narrow leaves and grows into tiny shrubs. The English thymes creep along the ground. 3 to 6 inches high. Perennial. The heady fragrance and flavor of thyme is a main ingredient of the bouquet garni of the French stock pot. Use it to flavor meats, stuffings and stews. Fresh leaves of thyme add a distinctive flavor to mayonnaise.

Resource Bibliography

GAMES

Indoor Games and Socials for Boys. Cornelius G. Baker. New York: Association Press, 1923.

Games and Sports. Arnold Arnold. New York: World Publishing, 1972.

The Book of Games. New York: Charles Scribners Sons, 1902.

The Sports and Pastimes of the People of England. Joseph Strutt. London: Methuen and Co., 1903.

American Non-Singing Games. Paul G. Brewster. Norman: University of Oklahoma Press, 1953.

Colonial Virginians at Play. Jane Carson. Charlottesville: The University of Virginia Press, 1965.

Games. George O. Draper. New York: Association Press, 1923.

America Learns to Play: A History of Popular Recreation, 1607-1940. Foster Rhea Dulles. Gloucester: Peter Smith, 1963.

Giant Book of Games. Frankel and Masters. New York: Sterling Publishing Co., 1956.

The Omnibus of Fun. Helen and Larry Eisenberg. New York: The Association Press, 1956.

The Fun Encyclopedia. E.O. Harbin. Nashville: The Cokesbury Press, 1950.

Social Games for Recreation. Bernard S. Mason and Elmer D. Mitchell. New York: A.S. Barnes and Co., 1938.

Traditional Games of England, Scotland, and Ireland, Vol. 2. Alice Gomme. New York: Dover Publications, 1965.

The Games Book for Boys and Girls. New York: E.P. Dutton & Co., 1900.

Child Life in Colonial Days. Alice Earle. Norwood: Macmillan Company, 1899.

Manly Games for Boys. Captain Crawley. London: William Tegg, 1873.

Handbook of Sporting Rules. George Benedict. Chicago and New York: Spalding Bros., 1886.

Games of the American Indian. Gordon Baldwin. London: W.W. Norton and Co., 1969.

Fun in the Water. Thomas Creton. New York: The Association Press, 1949.

The Art of Swimming. J. Frost. Rare Book Collection, Library of Congress. 1818.

Youthful Sports. J. Johnson. Rare Book Collection. 1802.

English Sports and Pastimes. Christina Hole. London: Batsford Ltd., 1949.

Games and Songs of American Children. William Wells Newell. New York: Dover Publications, 1965.

The Past of Pastimes. Vernon Bartlett. London: Chatto & Windus, 1969.

Board and Table Games. R.C. Bell. London: Oxford University Press, 1969.

Foster's Complete Hoyle. R.F. Foster. New York: J.B. Lippincott Co., 1953.

Yesterday's Games. Dr. Larry Freeman. Watkins Glen, N.Y.: Century House, 1970.

Handbook of Indoor Games and Stunts. D.A. Hindman. Englewood Cliffs, N.J.: Prentice Hall, Inc., 1955

A History of Board Games Other Than Chess. H.J.R. Murray. London: Oxford University Press, 1952.
Table Games: How to Make and How to Play Them. New York: A.S. Barnes and Co., 1939.

PARLOR GAMES

Dictionary of American History. James Truslow Adams, ed. New York: Charles Scribners Sons, 1940.
When Neighbors Were Neighbors: A Story of Love and Life in Olden Days. Galusha Anderson. Boston: Lothrop, Lee & Shepard Co., 1911.
Community Life Today and in Colonial Times. Daniel J. Beeby. New York: Charles E. Merrill Co., 1925.
Our Lusty Forefathers. Fairfax Downey. New York: Charles Scribners Sons, 1947.
Team-Work in Colonial Days. Walter K. Putney. Boston: W.A. Wilde Co., 1938.
Home Life in Colonial Days. Alice Morse Earl. New York: The Macmillan Co., 1898.
Let's Be Settlers With Daniel Boone. Peggy Parish. New York: Harper & Row, 1967.
Life in Colonial America. Elizabeth George Speare. New York: Chanticleer Press, Inc., 1963.

TOYS

Pageant of Toys. Mary Hiller. New York: Taplinger Publishing Co., 1965.
Children's Toys Through the Ages. Leslie Daiken. New York: Frederick A. Praeger, Inc., 1953.
Simple Toymaking. Sheila Jackson. New York: Watson-Guptill Publications, 1966.
European and American Dolls. Gwen White. New York: G.R. Putnam's Sons, 1966.
Dolls of Three Centuries. Eleanor St. George. New York: Charles Scribners Sons, 1951.
American Historical Dolls. Elizabeth Hooper. Baltimore: Elizabeth Hooper, 1941.
Dolls. John Noble. New York: Walker & Co., 1967.
Doll Making. Jean R. Laury. New York: Van Nostrand Co., 1970.

DRAMA

The Actor's Heritage. Walter P. Eaton. New York: Books for Libraries Press, 1924.
The American Playhouse in the Eighteenth Century. Edward McNamara. Cambridge: Harvard University Press, 1969.
The Making of the American Theatre. Howard Taubman. New York: Coward-McCann, Inc., 1967.
Three Hundred Years of American Drama and Theatre. Garff B. Wilson. Englewood Cliffs, N.J.: Prentice Hall, 1973.

PUPPETS

Puppet-Making. Chester J. Alkena. New York: Sterling Publishing Co., 1971.

Book of Puppetry. Remo Bufano. New York: Macmillan Co., 1955.
Punch and Judy: Its Origin and Evolution. Michael Bryan. Aberdeen: Waverly Press, 1972.
How to Make and Operate Marionettes. John C. Faustman. New York: J.C. Faustman, 1934.
Puppets in America, 1739 to Today. Paul McPharlin. Detroit: Plays, Inc., 1939.

MUSIC

A Williamsburg Songbook. John Edmunds. New York: Holt, Rinehart, and Winston, Inc., 1964.
"American Music," in *Harvard Dictionary of Music.* Willi Apel. Cambridge: Harvard University Press, 1961.
Folk Songs of North America. Alan Lomax. New York: Doubleday and Co., Inc. 1960.
Best Loved American Folk Songs. John Lomax, *et al.* New York: Grosset and Dunlap, 1947.
Musical Instruments in Eighteenth Century Virginia. Mary Goodwin. Williamsburg, Va.: Institute of Early American History and Culture.
Music in the United States: A Historical Introduction. H. Wiley Hitchcock. New York: Prentice Hall, 1969.
Music and Musicians in Early America. Irving Lowens. New York: Norton, 1964.
Music in a New Found Land. Wilfred Mellers. New York: Alfred A. Knopf, 1966.
The Puritans and Music in England and New England. Percy Scholes. New York: Russell and Russell, Inc., 1962.
Folk Dances and Singing Games. Elizabeth Burchenal. New York: S. Schirmer, Inc., 1933.
A Complete Guide to Social, Folk, and Square Dancing. Tillman J. Hall. Belmot, Calif.: Wadsworth Publishing Co., 1963.
American Indian Dances. John L. Squires and Robert E. McLean. New York: The Ronald Press Co., 1963.
The Traditional Tunes of the Child Ballads. Bertrand H. Bronson. Princeton: Princeton University Press, 1972.
Folk Songs of Old New England. Eloise Linscott. London: Archon Books, 1962.
American Favorite Ballads. Pete Seeger. New York: Oak Publications, 1971.

FLAG CEREMONIES

Flags of the U.S.A. David Eggenberger. New York: Thomas Y. Crowell Co., 1959.
Senior Girl Scout Handbook. Girl Scouts of America, 1963.
The History of the United States Flag. Milo M. Quaife. New York: Harper & Row, 1961.

CRAFTS

The Folk Arts and Crafts of New England. Priscilla Lord and Daniel J. Foley. New York: Chilton Co., 1965.
The Index of American Design. Erwin O. Christensen. New York: Macmillan Co., 1950.

Counted-Thread Embroidery. James Norbury. New York: Studio Publications, 1956.

Historical Needlework of Pennsylvania. Margaret B. Schiffer. New York: Charles Scribners Sons, 1968.

The Shuttle-Craft Book of American Weaving. Mary Atwater. New York: Macmillan Co., 1951.

America's Folk Art. Robert L. Polley. New York: G.P. Putnam's Sons, 1968.

How to Make Whirligigs and Whimmy Diddles. Florence H. Pettit. New York: Thomas Y. Crowell Co., 1972.

The Complete Book of Stencilcraft. Joann C. Day. New York: Simon and Schuster, 1974.

The Art of Stencil. Norman Labiberte and Alex Magelon. New York: Van Nostrand Reinhold Co., 1971.

How to Carve Characters in Wood. H.S. Anderson. Albuquerque: University of New Mexico Press, 1953.

Handbook of Handcarving and Whittling. Elsie Hanover. Cranbury: A.S. Barnes and Co., 1971.

Woodcarving Techniques and Projects. James B. Johnstone. Menlo Park: Lane Books, 1971.

Nature-Oriented Activities. Betty Vandersmissen. Ames: Iowa State University Press, 1965.

The Modern Art of Candle Creating. Don Olsen. New York: A.S. Barnes and Co., 1964.

Getting Started in Candlemaking. Walter E. Schultz. New York: Collier Books, 1972.

Contemporary Candlemaking. William E. Webster. Garden City: Doubleday and Co., 1972.

Woman's Day Book of American Needlework. Rose Lane. New York: Simon & Schuster, 1961.

Early American Textiles. Frances Little. New York: Century Co., 1931.

Antique Jewelry and Trinkets. Fred W. Burgess. Detroit: Singing Tree Press, 1972.

A History of Jewelry, 1100-1870. Joan Evans. London: Faber and Faber, 1970.

Jewelry, 1837-1901. Margaret Flower. New York: Walker and Co., 1968.

The Basketry Book. Mary Miles Blanchard. New York: Charles Scribners Sons, 1914.

Basket-Making for Amateurs. Phyllis Hosking. London: G. Bell and Sons, Ltd., 1960.

How to Make Baskets. Mary White. New York: Doubleday, Page and Co., 1901.

Quilting. Elizabeth King. New York: Leisure League, 1934.

Quilts and Coverlets: A Contemporary Approach. Jean R. Laury. New York: Van Nostrand Reinhold Co., 1971.

Quick and Easy Quilting. Bonnie Leman. Great Neck, N.Y.: Hearthside Press, 1972.

American Pieced Quilts. Jonathan Holstein. New York: Viking Press, 1972.

Quilting. Averil Colby. New York: Charles Scribners Sons, 1971.

FRAGRANCES

Potpourri, Incense, and Other Fragrant Concoctions. Ann Tucker. New York: Workman Publishing Co., 1972.

"Mix Your Own Colognes and Toilet Waters," *Family Circle* (July, 1973).

"Make Your Own Perfumes from Natural Oils," *Family Circle* (August, 1972).

FOOD

Grandmother in the Kitchen. Helen Lyon Adamson. New York: Crown Publishers, 1965

The Complete Book of Homemade Ice Cream, Milk Sherbet, and Sherbet. New York: St. Review Press, 1972.

The Great American Ice Cream Book. Paul Dickson. New York: Atheneum, 1972.

Living on the Earth. Alicia Laurel. New York: Vintage Books, 1970.

The Complete Book of Breads. Berneard Clayton, Jr. New York: Simon and Schuster, 1973.

Housekeeping in Old Virginia. Marion Cabell Tyree, ed. Kentucky: John P. Morton and Co., 1879.

Virginia Cookery, Past and Present. Woman's Auxiliary, Olivet Episcopal Church, Alexandria, Virginia, 1968.

Colonial Virginia Cookery. Jane Carson. Williamsburg, Va.: Colonial Williamsburg, Inc., 1968.

Old Cookery Books. W.C. Hazlitt. London: Elliot Stock, 1902.

Cooks, Gluttons, and Gourmets: A History of Cookery. E. Wason. New York: Doubleday and Co., 1962.

Index

Bibliography of Practical Books for Parents and Teachers

303 **SOCIAL STUDIES SKILLS TAUGHT THROUGH OBJECTIVES,** *by Mary Ann Williamson.*
303 social studies topics approached through objectives to teach and reinforce basic skills. Each objective is designed to be put into action in your classroom tomorrow. **$9.95** cloth (87491-036-6) **$6.95** paper (87491-037-4).

INVITATION TO LEARNING, VOL. I: LEARNING CENTER HANDBOOK, *by Ralph Voight.*
A "how-to" manual for understanding and implementing learning centers in your classroom. "The author offers practical hints and tips to get the learning center approach started in a classroom." U.S. Office of Ed ERIC Resume. **$4.95** paper (87491-318-7).

INVITATION TO LEARNING, VOL. II: CENTER TEACHING WITH INSTRUCTIONAL DEPTH, *by Ralph Voight.*
A manual of special learning center techniques and methods, more than 60 "child-tested" station examples, fully illustrated for easy adaptation to any classroom. **$4.95** paper (87491-382-9).

INVITATION TO LEARNING, VOL. III: 30 COMPLETE CENTERS WITH 101 CHARACTER CUTOUTS AND ILLUSTRATIONS, *by Ralph Voight.*
Beautiful, ready to cut and paste artwork (over 100 charming, colorful illustrations) and over 30 ideas with complete directions for creating self-contained learning centers. **$9.95** paper (87491-339-3).

INVITATION TO LEARNING, VOL. IV . . . MAGIC! A LEARNING CENTER SOURCEBOOK, *by Windley.*
How to set up a magic learning center, complete with 65 magic tricks to experience with your students and to reinforce learning in these areas: perception, science, math, skill, creativity, memory, fun, holidays. **$9.95** cloth (87491-035-8), **$6.95** paper (87491-038-2).